Talking
Films
and
Songs

Talking Films and Songs

Javed Akhtar

in conversation with

Nasreen Munni Kabir

OXFORD
UNIVERSITY PRESS

OXFORD
UNIVERSITY PRESS

Oxford University Press is a department of the University of Oxford.
It furthers the University's objective of excellence in research, scholarship,
and education by publishing worldwide. Oxford is a registered trademark of
Oxford University Press in the UK and in certain other countries.

Published in India by
Oxford University Press
22 Workspace, 2nd Floor, 1/22 Asaf Ali Road, New Delhi 110 002, India

First Edition published in 2018
Fourth impression 2023

ISBN-13 (print edition): 978-0-19-948211-5
ISBN-10 (print edition): 0-19-948211-X

ISBN-13 (eBook): 978-0-19-909177-5
ISBN-10 (eBook): 0-19-909177-3

Typeset in Perpetua 12.5/15
by Tranistics Data Technologies, New Delhi 110 044
Printed in India by Repro India Limited

Contents

Contents

Preface

The book, *Talking Films*, began with a casual conversation that took place between a friend, Rukun Advani, and myself at the India International Centre (the famous and wonderful IIC) in Delhi sometime in the late 1990s. We met for coffee and talked about different book ideas. Rukun knew that *Movie Mahal*, the series I had made on Hindi cinema for the UK's Channel 4 TV in the 1980s, included interviews with many of India's best known film-makers and actors, and he suggested that I think of using these interviews as a basis for a book project.

The first person who came to mind was Javed Akhtar. His intelligence and wit stand out, as anyone who has met him will attest. To me, his larger-than-life personality was evident when we first met on 23 April 1987 at the Sun-n-Sand Hotel in Mumbai during the filming of *Movie Mahal*.

Since then, we met many times, including an occasion in 1989, when Javed Saab spoke about Amitabh Bachchan for my documentary *Follow That Star*. Astutely, he situated Vijay, the hero that Amitabh Bachchan played, in the social context of India in the 1970s—a persona that he himself had created with Salim Khan. This writing duo, known as Salim-Javed, has left a deep and lasting mark on Hindi cinema. Their powerful screenplays and clever, multi-layered dialogue have brought them recognition that extends far beyond the frontiers of India. From the 1970s on, this celebrated duo was instrumental in taking Hindi cinema in a new and different direction.

Sometime in 1998, I went to see Javed Saab in his beautiful ocean-facing apartment in Juhu and proposed that we do a book together. Perhaps because he had seen my work and had particularly liked the documentary that I had made called *In Search of Guru Dutt* that he immediately agreed, and the work began.

We recorded our conversations on a tiny tape recorder as we sat in the compact room that was his study. This was before his home was refurbished, after which he moved to a much larger space that became his office. When he spoke about cinema, his analysis was unlike anything I had heard before, or have heard since. We talked for many hours in his Juhu flat, and because I lived in London, and continue to do so, our sessions were spread over a year. I believe we met at least twenty times for about two hours at a time.

Seeing Javed Saab's life from afar, it was difficult to gauge just how busy a life he was leading, and since the late 1990s the pace has only intensified. There was always some pressing deadline to meet and even in those days, the phones never stopped ringing and visitors constantly streamed in and out. Shabana Azmi was also very busy, but she would occasionally pop her head round the door of the study to ask if we needed anything to drink or eat. All the stopping and starting did not really disturb Javed Saab's train of thought and his unwavering focus on the task at hand was remarkable. His sense of humour seamlessly underscored his very serious and keenly observed thoughts and ideas on India and Indian film-making. He also shared personal incidents in his life with wit and intelligence.

At the end of the year, when our conversations had been transcribed, Javed Saab and I sat together and read the whole text to see if it all made sense. The manuscript was approved, sent to the publisher, and then on to the printing press.

Book launches have now become frenetic and star-studded affairs, but those were the pioneering years of publications on Indian cinema in the English language, and our book launch was simple, yet elegant. It took place at the Y.B. Chavan Hall in Mumbai on 23 July 1999. Shabana Azmi read selected passages from the book, and our chief guest, Aamir Khan, officially released *Talking Films: Conversation on Hindi Cinema with Javed Akhtar*. When it was Javed Saab's turn to speak, he started off by saying with a smile, 'When Nasreen talked to me about doing a book with her, she was making me an offer that I couldn't refuse.'

In the months—now years—that followed since the release of *Talking Films*, the enduring and enthusiastic response to the book from academics and cinema lovers the world over has been most gratifying. While aiming to present a slice of cinema history, the text offers a groundbreaking approach to the understanding of Hindi films. It is true that *Talking Films* was written in the flow of intense and energized conversations, and this has been much appreciated by its readers. Perhaps that is why cinema fans and scholars alike say that the book is now a must-read text on Hindi cinema.

In 2005, we decided to continue our collaboration with another book: *Talking Songs*. It was a great personal delight to be back again in the company of Javed Akhtar, with his astute and analytical mind, his ever sharp intelligence, and his unfailing sense of humour. Through our continuing conversations, Javed Saab turned his attention to what gives Hindi/Urdu film songs such distinctive expressions of thought and emotion that mean so much for many millions. In addition to his insights on film lyrics and lyricists, we discussed the craft, intuition, and emotion that informed Javed Saab's own songwriting. Sitting in his study, with the phone ringing constantly, and endless interruptions, Javed Akhtar has plucked from his imagination words that some months later have defined for us the intensity of new love or described the perils of war. His countless songs have entered our psyche, sometimes mirroring, sometimes defining a fountain of feelings.

The publication of *Talking Songs* coincided with Javed Akhtar's sixtieth birthday in 2005, and Shah Rukh Khan kindly released the book in Mumbai. Once again, Javed Saab's distinctive voice and insider's perspective engaged readers, encouraging them to think about songwriting in a new and fresh light.

As time passed, I thought it would be wonderful to have a combined version of both books. I approached Oxford University Press (OUP) India with the idea, and they were most enthusiastic, and agreed to the publishing of an omnibus version. Any subject repetitions and overlaps in *Talking Films* and *Talking Songs* have been removed and minor updating has been undertaken. Even though the conversations are about an earlier era, Javed Akhtar's thoughts and ideas are just as relevant today, and I am sure they will remain so in times to come.

As we publish this edition of the two books as *Talking Films and Songs*, I would once again like to thank all those who have helped with the original books. Special thanks for this edition goes to Baba Azmi, Peter Chappell, Carrol De Souza, Shonali Gajwani, and Oxford University Press India. My deepest gratitude goes to Shabana Azmi for her lively introduction to *Talking Songs*, which I am happy to say features in this new edition as well. As many of the events we talked about date to the period prior to the renaming of Bombay as Mumbai, Calcutta as Kolkata, and Madras as Chennai, I have used the original city names for consistency.

These conversations were a delight to work on, and although many years have now passed, whenever I pick up either of these books and start reading, quite honestly, I have not been able to put them down. They still feel fresh and engaging and have, in a sense, taken on a life of their own—so much so that I now feel an outsider to the whole process. Sometimes words and thoughts just flow of their own accord and I think that is what happened here.

Nasreen Munni Kabir
17 September 2017

TALKING FILMS

NASREEN MUNNI KABIR [NMK]: What is the heart of a good conversation?

JAVED AKHTAR [JA]: Conversations have three levels: people, incidents, and ideas. The lowest form of conversation is about people. When we go up one rung, we reach incidents, and these have a slightly larger spectrum than talking about people. But the conversation that really matters is when we talk about ideas, because ideas are universal and live beyond time and space.

NMK: Could you tell me how you define the difference between film dialogue and conversation?

JA: We must understand that a film has a time limit. We have to cover A to Z within, say, 90 minutes—so that's a limitation. It's like giving a speech or participating in a debate in which you have to make all your points within six minutes or so. In a film, you have 90 minutes to narrate the whole story. So you have to be economical with your words. Billy Wilder has aptly said, 'Film dialogue should be like a poor man's telegram.' This is true of the way most scenes are written, but sometimes you have to indulge in rhetoric. Particularly in Indian cinema—that's a requirement of the script and of cinema itself. But I consider film dialogue as edited and directed conversation. You shouldn't be allowed to meander. Good film dialogue is not conversation but a kind of representation of it.

NMK: Do you remember having heard a conversation that you've reworked into dialogue?

JA: I suppose I have done that. I've taken the raw material from real conversations, expressions, styles of talking, pauses, the peculiarities of sentence structures. Just like everyone has their own way of walking, sitting, or turning, everyone has their own stresses while speaking, and everyone's sentence

---

structure varies. How do I express something? Take the same line of speech and get three people to say it: each person will say it in a different manner. A sensitive dialogue writer notices this, and when he's writing dialogue, he decides how a character will speak. He constructs the lines with particular pauses, stresses, and so on.

NMK: So dialogue is a kind of gateway to understanding screen characters, and the way they speak tells us something about them, for instance, in the choice of words they use and so on.

JA: I believe words are like people. You scrutinize them carefully. You're sitting here, the door opens, and someone enters. The first thing you notice is the appearance of the person; then you're introduced. You discover he's an engineer or a chartered accountant. He sits down and you start talking. Soon you find common links. He's an engineer, so he belongs to a certain class, and he's from such and such city. Oh, so he knows your cousin's friend, and so on. You develop a kind of association with him and you try to slot him. In the same way, take a word that is unfamiliar to you—the first thing that touches you is the sound of the word, the physical appearance of it. Then comes its occupation and meaning. The dictionary provides its occupation and conveys the meaning. That's the job of this word. But that's not the only thing. The word, in fact, has other associations. You start thinking, where did you meet it before, what kind of company does it keep? Where is it from? What kind of moral values does it represent? A good writer is supposed to be aware of three things before using a word: its physical appearance, its occupation, and the associations it evokes.

NMK: When you were growing up, did films or books have a greater impact on you?

JA: Books. Books. In my formative years, I hadn't seen many films; books were more easily available. And there was a tradition of reading in the family; everybody read. There would be lots of books and magazines in the house, and people would discuss them. So I read a lot. Films were expensive, one could see two films in a month; oh no, perhaps one film a month. But we could read as many books as we wanted.

NMK: Were these books in Urdu or English or Hindi?

JA: Most of my early reading was in Urdu. I remember, I read my first novel in English when I was perhaps fifteen.

NMK: Do you remember what book it was?

JA: *Inqilaab* by K.A. Abbas.

NMK: That was a sophisticated choice for such a young person.

JA: I had read Gorki's *Mother* in an Urdu translation when I was perhaps thirteen. All these writers—Gogol, Chekhov, and Pushkin—I had read them all in Urdu by the time I was fifteen.

NMK: Did their worlds seem alien to you, or did you find they showed you a world that you could identify with?

JA: I read page after page, without fully understanding what was being said. But I believed that if I kept reading, I would understand. So, in that way, you could say my concentration is good.

NMK: This obviously shows you have a deep sense of curiosity.

JA: I have read so many books that I understood only much later in life. I read a lot of poetry and could recall the lines. And a lot of fiction, including Bengali literature—a lot of Bengali literature was available in Urdu translation. There was a galaxy of Urdu writers at that time, including Krishan Chander, Rajinder Singh Bedi, Ismat Chughtai, and Saadat

Hasan Manto. I was not allowed to read Manto till I was at college—he was considered taboo.

NMK: Why?

JA: Because Manto used to deal with topics bordering sex.

NMK: So that was considered outrageous?

JA: That was outrageous. [smiles] So I read Manto when I was in college. I was a serious fan of Krishan Chander's. Like a teenager would be of some film star.

NMK: Had you ever met him?

JA: When I came to Bombay [now Mumbai], I did meet him. I wouldn't say we became friends, because he was much older. But I was very close to him.

NMK: Do you think it's a good thing to meet someone that you admire?

JA: Why not? Sometimes you can be disappointed. That's natural too. If you admire somebody from a distance, you make an image of him or her, and you fall in love with that image. Soon you are no longer in love with that person—you are in love with the image you've created. And that image is the extension of your own fantasies, so that image is finally you. It's a kind of self-love. [laughs] Soon you forget that person and get very upset if he or she does not match up to your fantasy. Bhai, it's not right. I think if you're a grown-up, mature and objective, you have to understand that people are not your fantasy. People are people after all.

NMK: What about the other authors you read in your adolescence? Which writer did you particularly like?

JA: Ibn-e-Safi. He was very good in every way—his style of writing, his diction, his sense of humour. It is very unfortunate that Urdu literature and Urdu critics have not given him his due.

It is a kind of cultural insecurity that we don't have the guts to appreciate things that don't fall under conventional ideas of art. You need a Satyajit Ray to say that *Sholay* is a very good film. But an average film critic was hesitant to say so. In the same way, I don't think Asia was—or is—capable of creating a Charlie Chaplin. It can't.

NMK: Why not?

JA: Because for that you have to accept that humour is respectable. Humour is a very serious thing. I don't know why we have a strange highbrow attitude towards comedy in our country. We think humour is cheap and inferior. I think we have been deprived of happiness and pleasure for a very long time, so we think that anything that can make people happy or can provide pleasure is either sinful or taboo, or of inferior quality. It is believed that things that are respectable have to be bitter, unpleasant, heavy, and boring. I don't know why.

NMK: What kind of humour did Ibn-e-Safi have? Did he use irony?

JA: No. He used to write thrillers like James Hadley Chase or Earl Stanley Gardner. He was the first person that I am aware of who had a kind of Western sophistication in his writing and combined it with all the richness of the Urdu language. He had the understatement and crispness that you find in American novels.

NMK: Did his work share that special kind of pace which is prevalent in American thrillers?

JA: Yes! It was wonderful. And Ibn-e-Safi was very popular. Millions of people were addicted to him. He used to write *Jaasoosi Duniya* [Spy World]—that was the name of the series. Ibn-e-Safi was from Allahabad. I knew people who knew him, but I had never met him personally. He later lived in

Karachi, and has since passed away. I haven't read his books for years.

NMK: Were his detectives living in a big city?

JA: Yes. They were a team. There were two detectives: Colonel Fareedi and Captain Hameed. [laughs] Colonel Ahmed Kamal Fareedi. Oh my god, they were such fascinating characters, and his villains were so fascinating, too. Ibn-e-Safi was a master at naming his characters. Those of us who have read him can never forget those names.

NMK: What was special about them?

JA: Strange names. There was a Chinese villain named Sing-Hi; and a Portuguese villain called Garson—so unusual for the 1950s and early 1960s. Another of his characters was an Englishman who had come to India and was into some kind of yoga and all that. His name was Gerald Shastri. Ibn-e-Safi had created a whole world—gradually you became familiar with his characters and the places they inhabited.

NMK: Where were the stories set? In which city?

JA: In an imaginary place. But the reader became familiar with the roads, avenues, and streets of that imaginary place. Colonel Ahmed Kamal Fareedi was actually from a royal family, but he wanted to work, so he became a detective. The title 'Colonel' was an honorary title that was given to him. Colonel Fareedi had a huge library, and he was some kind of an anthropologist. He was a very rich man; he had a very big house and many dogs. He was also fond of snakes and had many in his home. He could speak every language that existed. What a wonderful man he was.

NMK: A dreamer and an adventurer.

JA: He was Sherlock Holmes and James Bond rolled into one. He had a huge following.

NMK: With all the reading that you have done, have you ever thought of adapting a novel to the screen?

JA: [*long pause*] I have never thought about it. Let me think. [*humming under breath*] I can't remember the name of the author, but when I was at college, I read this novel called *If I Forget Thee*. I was fascinated by it. The novel was set in Jerusalem in Roman times. It's the story of a young man and his blind father who live on the outskirts of Rome. On the day that the young man is given a toga, the symbol of being considered an adult, his father tells him that he is really half Roman and half Jewish. Now this boy is in love with the daughter of the Jewish high priest in Jerusalem, so that creates conflict. It was a very dramatic love story: this boy and girl, and the dilemma of the boy—whether he's a Roman or a Jew. When he decides that he should become a Jew, other Jews do not accept him, and the Romans do not accept him either. It was a much better story than *Ben Hur*. I used to fantasize about what a beautiful film the book would make.

NMK: What kind of impact do you feel a book has, compared to a film?

JA: Most of the time when I've read a book and then seen it adapted to the screen, I have been disappointed. It is not because film is an inferior medium; it's not that. But when you're reading a book, you're participating. The images that are being formed are somewhere between the description in the text and the imagination of the reader. Readers take the information, the data from the novel, and create their own images. So obviously, they are perfect for them. When watching a film, you don't participate—you are given everything. The menu is fixed—take it or leave it. You don't have a say; you're just a spectator. You read a novel like *Dracula* and you see the film. The film has visuals, music, and sound effects, while the novel has nothing, only words written on paper. Yet the kind of atmosphere of fear that the novel creates, the film cannot, in spite of all those effects. That's the difference, and that is where a novel has an edge over a film.

NMK: I'm thinking of *The Silence of the Lambs*; the novel is far more terrifying.

JA: Naturally, because when you read it, you are the director, you are the cameraman, and the editor. So, obviously, you will like your own film better. [*both laugh*] While you are reading the novel, you also do the casting, decide the frame compositions and locations, and design the sets. I have noticed something, the sets in a novel seem to be made of some kind of adaptable material. In one scene, you imagine the room this way, and in another scene that takes place in the same location, the room changes according to your convenience. Where would you have this facility in cinema?

NMK: Do you remember the first film you saw as a child? Was it in Lucknow?

JA: I must have been three years old when I saw my first film. I sat on the lap of some lady, and I only remember one scene of the film. I used to quiz people about this particular scene, and years later, I discovered that the film was *Nagina*, with Nutan and Nasir Khan. Nutan was perhaps fourteen years old when she did the film. But the first film that I was conscious of seeing and that I remember seeing was *Aan*.

NMK: That's interesting. One of the first films I ever saw was also Mehboob Khan's *Aan*. I still have memories of seeing the film in London——I remember shots of Nimmi running through yellow mustard fields singing 'Aaj mere mann mein sakhi bansuri' [I hear the sound of the flute in my heart]. How old were you when you saw *Aan*?

JA: I was admitted to Class I in the morning, and that evening I saw the film at Basant Talkies in Lucknow. I must have been seven or eight. I was vaguely aware of this name, Dilip Kumar, but I was not very sure who he was, what he looked like, and whether I had seen him before. But when I saw *Aan*, I came to know this is Dilip Kumar.

NMK: Did you enjoy the film?

JA: It was an enjoyable film. There were horses and swords and fights and songs, and Dilip Kumar was very good.

NMK: Did you find cinema itself magical?

JA: Oh yes! As a kid, I was fascinated by cinema, and when I was twelve or thirteen, I wanted to become a film star. I used to read a lot and sing film songs in my childhood. One thing I've noticed, Munni, we might believe that we do things merely on the spur of the moment, but unconsciously, in fact, we're preparing ourselves for the future—and this is true of the experience of many. Two things have helped me in my life: my deep interest in literature and my extreme fascination for films—I was glamour-struck by cinema.

NMK: Films in India have a huge influence. Was this also true of the 1950s and 1960s when you were growing up?

JA: In the 1950s and 1960s, people were tremendously involved with cinema, and when they'd see a film, they would react very strongly. In those days, films had more defined genres. For example, we used to have stunt films with stars like Fearless Nadia, Kamran, Ranjan, Sheikh Mukhtar, and Dara Singh. The audience for these films was very boisterous—they would shout and jump about as they watched the action and they'd express extreme pleasure when the hero would beat up the villain. But now, the stunt film no longer exists as a separate category in Indian cinema.

NMK: Which were the films that moved you emotionally at that time?

JA: *Do Bigha Zameen, Jagriti*. Have you seen *Jagriti*?

NMK: No, I don't believe so.

JA: *Jagriti* was a very successful film made by Filmistan. Abhi Bhattacharya played a teacher, a warden. And the story revolves around his relationship with the children in his care. Some are very complex, some are lovelorn or poor, and others are rebellious.

NMK: What did you like about *Jagriti*?

JA: Perhaps, I identified with the film because it had many children of my age; and then the hero was a misunderstood, lovelorn boy, so I identified with him—I felt that I was like that too. The teacher in the film was a kind of a father figure who was really a wonderful person. At that age, you admire those kinds of characters. I liked the atmosphere, with many children living together in a hostel, playing practical jokes and having fun. There was a child who was from a poor family who walked on crutches, and another boy would sing, 'Chalo chalen Ma' [Mother, let us make our way]. I think I cried a lot in that film. I also liked *Jaal* very much.

NMK: Guru Dutt's film? Did you see it at the time of its release in 1952? You must have been very young.

JA: No, I saw *Jaal* later at an exhibition at the Engineering College in Aligarh. I came to know there was a film show on the first floor, and the ticket cost a rupee. [*laughs*] Somehow, I managed to get a ticket—I don't know who bought it for me—and I saw *Jaal*.

NMK: Was that the first Guru Dutt film you saw?

JA: Perhaps, perhaps. *Jaal* definitely created a deep impression on me. I think this fascination for the negative hero started with

Jaal because I had a kind of rebellious spirit. All of us admire people who can stand up and say, 'No, I won't accept this.' That's why we are fascinated by characters like the Crimson Pirate, Robin Hood, Phoolan Devi, and dacoits like Mansingh or Behram. These people are like Tony, the character in *Jaal*, who was a crook and a smuggler. This kind of anti-hero was very unusual in Indian cinema of the time. Today if you say the hero is a smuggler, it's a cliché—oh no, not again!

I believe *Jaal* didn't do well, but I will never forget it because the film was ahead of its time. Dev Anand, who played Tony, had this total disregard for morality and ignored all sense of decency. Dev Anand had always been a nice man on screen; sometimes he played the role of a pickpocket or gangster, but there was no bitterness in his characters. His roles were mostly glamorous and superficial. But *Jaal* was Guru Dutt's film, and his hero didn't care to be considered a good man. At the end of the film, Tony is seen to repent and that too was very subtly done. All we see is that he will not shoot the girl he loves in order to save himself.

NMK: I've often thought that there was a link between Vijay of *Deewaar* and Tony of *Jaal*. These negative heroes are of the same family. What about the famous screen anti-hero, Birju, in *Mother India*?

JA: I remember that I saw *Mother India* in 1957 when I was twelve or thirteen. Both Birju and Tony left a very deep impression on me. I remember Balraj Sahni in *Do Bigha Zameen* too, but I liked Birju.

NMK: Would you have preferred the character Balraj Sahni plays in *Do Bigha Zameen* to revolt?

JA: Perhaps, perhaps. Not that I compared them and rejected Balraj Sahni as a result—that didn't happen. But Birju made a deeper impression on me.

NMK: More than Radha, the character Nargis played in *Mother India*?

JA: I would not say that. As a matter of fact, I have been a great fan of Nargis. The first film of hers I saw was *Shree 420*. I was fascinated by her and saw some kind of a mother figure in her. Since my mother had died when I was very young, there was a kind of longing in me for a mother, and Nargis used to fit that image.

NMK: Was it your mother or your father who named you? How did you get the name 'Javed'?

JA: That's a very interesting story. I was born on 17 January 1945 in Gwalior at the Kamla Hospital—Kamla is perhaps the name of Madhavrao Scindia's grandmother. My father and his friends came to the hospital straight from the Communist Party office, and as they sat looking at the baby and talking about it, somebody said, 'Do you know that when a child is born in a Muslim family, the azan is read in his ears?' My father's friends said, 'But we have a different faith and we have different beliefs, so what do we do?' My father, who was holding the *Communist Manifesto* in his hand, replied, 'All right, we'll read this to him.' So the *Communist Manifesto* was read in my ear. [*NMK laughs*]

Then they discussed what my name should be. Someone reminded my father that when he married my mother, Safia [Safia Siraj-ul Haq], he had written a poem that included the line, 'Lamha-lamha kisi jaadoo ka fasaana hoga' [Every moment will have a magical story]. Why not name him Jaadu [magic]?

NMK: How lovely!

JA: So they called me Jaadu, and for quite some time, I was only known as Jaadu. But when it was decided that I should go to kindergarten or whatever, people said that Jaadu wasn't a serious name. By then Jaadu had become established as my name, so they had to find a name that sounded similar. That's how they arrived at 'Javed'. Generally, the pet name is derived from the real name; in my case, it was the reverse.

NMK: And what does 'Javed' mean?

JA: Javed means 'immortal'. If you're asking the meaning of my surname, then I must tell you that Akhtar means 'star'. *[both laugh]*

NMK: 'The immortal star'. That's really who you are. Who still calls you Jaadu? I know Shabana does, but do other people?

JA: Oho! My whole family and all my old friends and school friends called me Jaadu—I was never known as 'Javed', only as 'Jaadu'. In Bombay, all my old associates still call me Jaadu, even Shaukat Apa [Shaukat Azmi]. She doesn't call me Javed, neither does my brother.

NMK: Did the reading of the *Communist Manifesto* in your ear have any effect on your later life?

JA: Maybe my atheism has something to do with it.

NMK: Are you a complete atheist?

JA: I genuinely believe that in two hundred years from now, this period will be considered the strangest time in human history. In the days when people and the clergy believed that the sun moved around the earth, they were ignorant but not crazy. They really believed it. But a man who might work in NASA or walk on the moon and then go to church on Sundays is schizophrenic. For an educated person living in the twentieth century, faith and scientific reality are contradictory.

NMK: Can we go back to your family? Do tell me a bit more about your parents.

JA: I'll give you a life sketch in a nutshell. My parents were both from UP [Uttar Pradesh]. My father's family came from Khairabad, which is about 80 miles from Lucknow, and my mother's family from Rudauli—some 80 or 100 miles from Lucknow.

My father's family were scholars and writers. My great-great-grandfather, Fazl-e Haq Khairabadi, was Ghalib's contemporary and a very close friend of his. A scholar in logic, philosophy, religion, and literature, Fazl-e Haq also edited Ghalib's *Deewaan*. Ghalib was a poet who was much ahead of his time. In his day, there was no tradition of editing a book of poetry, but Ghalib gave this book to Fazl-e Haq to edit as he had a lot of respect for my great-great-grandfather's intellect. He was a man of many facets—some of his books are available in the Chicago University library and form part of the syllabus in Egypt. He was considered an authority on religion too. He took an active part in the 1857 freedom movement and was arrested and sent to the Andamans, where he died. His daughter, Hirma, was a nineteenth-century poet.

NMK: I am sure there were very few women in India who were poets at the time.

JA: But Hirma was. Her husband was also a poet. They had two sons, Bismil and Muztar, both poets. Muztar [Khairabadi] was the younger son and he was my grandfather. Many of his poems are extremely famous—he wrote every kind of poetry and not only the ghazal but also the qasida, kajri, hori, thumri, and the geet in Hindi as well. One of his kajris, 'Chha rahi kaali ghata jiyara mora ghabraaye hai' [The gathering dark clouds fill me with unrest], was sung by Begum Akhtar. He was a sessions judge in Gwalior State and that is where my father was born—in Gwalior.

NMK: So your father was brought up in a world filled with poets and poetry?

JA: There was poetry all around, and he himself started writing poems at fourteen. My grandfather died when my father was fifteen or sixteen years old—and that is when my father was sent to Aligarh to study. There he met other young poets of the time like Majaz, Jazbi and Ali Sardar Jafri. In the 1930s, they were all active members of the Progressive Writers' Movement, which was a liberal leftist movement—these poets helped change the mood and style of poetry. Until that time poetry was considered, to a great extent, as art for art's sake—excepting for people like Hali, one of Ghalib's disciples, who wrote poetry that had a strong social message. There was of course a socio-political consciousness in the poetry of Ghalib and Mir, but it took a very indirect and subtle form. But I'm talking about poetry that was primarily used to convey certain social messages and fight for causes, like the work of Dr Allama Iqbal. The Progressive Writers' Movement in Urdu was the natural organic growth of that mood. That was the time when communism was rising on the horizon and making inroads in Southeast and South Asia. These poets were leftist and communists, and they started writing poetry with a certain socio-political commitment.

One of the poets who belonged to the Progressive Writers' Movement was Majaz. He was my mother's brother, and it was through him that my parents had met. My mother was also a writer and had studied at Aligarh University. My parents married and lived for a time in Gwalior in the mid-1940s. At that time, my father was teaching Urdu at Victoria College, where the famous Hindi poet Shivmangal Singh 'Suman' was teaching Hindi. One of their students was Atal Bihari Vajpayee, our former prime minister.

NMK: When did your parents move to Bhopal from Gwalior?

JA: When I was about two years old. The Communist Party had a certain impact in India and attracted many people, including writers and poets. My father was a Party member and he was also president of the Progressive Writers' Movement

Association. He was forced to go underground, and left for Bombay. My mother stayed on in Bhopal and was teaching at Hamidiya College. So my brother and I lived with our mother, and she brought us up until she fell very ill with scleroderma, an autoimmune disease. My brother, Salman and I then went to live with my maternal grandparents in Lucknow. On 18 January 1953, when I was eight, my mother died.

NMK: She died a day after your eighth birthday. And how old was your brother?

JA: He is one and a half years younger, so he was six and a half when our mother died. Salman now lives in Philadelphia and is a highly respected psychoanalyst. A few years ago, an American medical journal listed a hundred top doctors in the US and he was among them. He writes poetry in Urdu and English and has been published in both languages. He writes a lot about his own work and travels all around. He is also a visiting professor at Harvard.

NMK: Were you close as children?

JA: I wouldn't say that. We were brothers, of course, but after a couple of years, my aunt, who also lived with us in Lucknow, moved to Aligarh, so I went to stay with her. While I studied in Aligarh, Salman continued to live in Lucknow with our grandparents. I did my matriculation in Aligarh and then my father took me to Bhopal.

NMK: And how old were you then?

JA: Fifteen.

NMK: So you hardly knew your father?

JA: No. We had some kind of image of him because my mother used to tell us so much about him. My father would visit us sometimes, and I have very vague memories of seeing him when I was a kid. I must have been five or six at the time, so there are some images, but I don't remember many details of the time.

NMK: Do you have any memories of your mother?

JA: I was eight when she died. I do remember her. A child of eight remembers a lot. In psychiatry, it's believed that by the age of seven, your personality is signed, sealed, and delivered.

NMK: Did the influences on your character come from your mother, as you were close to her?

JA: Young children are close to their mothers, and so was I. I think she was very fond of me. My parents were married for nine years but most of that time they didn't live together. My father published all the letters that she had written to him—it was an extremely popular book, and since 1954–5, almost every year, one or two editions of her book of letters are reprinted. She was an avid letter writer and wrote almost every day.

NMK: I assume she signed her work as Safia Akhtar. What is her book called?

JA: Zer-e-Lab [Under the Lip]. She made a place for herself in Urdu literature because of those letters. They were published after she died.

NMK: Did she write about you?

JA: In many letters, she writes to my father, 'this is his first day at school', 'he did this or that', or 'the teacher gave him this report'. You can see that she thought she had a little genius. Like most mothers, she was quite proud of her son. [laughs]

NMK: Is there anything in those letters that surprised you about her reading of your character?

JA: I was quite surprised to see how accurately she had described me when I was about six and a half. I once read the letter to Shabana, and she was also quite amazed at what my mother wrote: 'This boy has tremendous control and command over Urdu and is rather hesitant in English. He is extremely talkative but not very practical.' She described me as someone who makes big plans but doesn't do anything about them. And that's describing a boy who was under seven years old. I'm much the same even today. [both smile]

NMK: Maybe that's why your father was surprised that you had indeed made something of your life. You know, sometimes, when a child is very imaginative, parents fear that he or she may not do so well in the real world.

JA: Maybe. But I suppose every mother believes she has one very brilliant child!

NMK: Her death must have been devastating for you.

JA: It must have been. It's difficult for me to analyse it now, but I am quite sure it must have been hard for a child of that age to lose both parents—one to life and another to death. It can be shocking. And to realize that all your life you have been living in someone else's house, it may be your grandfather's home or your aunt's home, but it is not your home. When I was in Bhopal, I lived in hostels and then with friends. When I was nineteen I came to Bombay, but I did not get on with my father, so I lived on my own. Perhaps because we had lived apart for so long, there were many unresolved misunderstandings and hurts. Then he got married again, and I didn't get on with my stepmother.

NMK: When your mother died, did you dream about her?

JA: Yes. I remember a dream that used to trouble me in my childhood. The last time I saw her, she was wrapped in a white shroud. For months, I had this recurring dream of a white shroud, and it used to frighten me. Somehow this image came in my dreams.

NMK: Was she in the shroud?

JA: No, it was just the shroud. It walked around—that used to frighten me. I wasn't even sure it was my mother. Yes, it was a shroud, it wasn't her.

NMK: Perhaps it was death.

JA: Perhaps.

NMK: When do you think the friction between you and your father became obvious? Was it open hostility?

JA: Oh yes. It started when I was fifteen. By the time I was seventeen, I was living with a friend. My father didn't know where I was. When I came to Bombay, I stayed in my father's house for the first five or six days—that's all. I don't hold it against him because I think he was a very shy and withdrawn person, and in our country, we don't have a strong tradition of bonding between father and son anyway. There is awkwardness even in so-called normal households. I think it's changing now because of the nuclear family—people living in big cities are obliged to share smaller and smaller spaces. A physical nearness is unavoidable, and you just can't pretend to be unaware of each other's existence. Otherwise, traditionally, fathers and sons have had very awkward relationships. In spite of that, I remember many occasions when he spoke to me as a friend because he was a writer and a leftist and a liberal person. Once he even told me about a certain lady who had been in his life before he had met my mother. He talked about the misgivings in our social circle about that particular relationship. He told me this story in great detail, when I must have been about seventeen. I can remember times when he spoke about poetry or literature or writing, and those conversations definitely did leave an impression on me. I suppose I wanted to pretend that I didn't care; perhaps I used that as a kind of defence mechanism because if I had admitted that I cared, it might have hurt more.

NMK: Did you feel abandoned by your father? He could have stayed with you, especially when your mother died.

JA: While my mother was alive, she never let us feel abandoned by him. She always made us proud of our father, who was a great poet, a communist. She explained that he was not at home because of this great cause and so on. We used to hero-worship him, but after she died and we started living with our maternal relatives, I did feel let down by him. And that created a kind of resentment in me—a kind of anger and a 'who-cares?' attitude. I never showed my hurt. Never. I developed a facility for getting on with people—it might have been a necessary defence at that time, but it came in handy later on. Even as a child, I had to have good PR, and so I was a very popular child, even in my schooldays.

NMK: Was it your intelligence that charmed people?

JA: Perhaps. Or my sense of humour—it worked, it did work.

NMK: Do you think it was purely a survival technique?

JA: Both. Everybody finds a survival technique that matches his or her personality. Even if you are out to sell yourself to others, you can only offer what you have in your repertoire. I was known to be an interesting conversationalist and a boy with a sense of humour, and as a result, I was very popular at school and later at college. For at least four years, it was my friends from Bhopal who looked after me.

NMK: Financially as well?

JA: Oh yes, for four years I lived off my friends. Sometimes I lived with one friend and sometimes with another. My clothes, my books, my next meal would come from them.

NMK: So you had no home?

JA: There was no home. After the age of six or seven, I never had a real home until I bought one many years later.

NMK: How do you think that affected you?

JA: Life is strange. Sometimes if you look back, Munni, you feel like editing your life, rewriting it. You change scene 12, but the story is so well-knit, the moment you change scene 12, which is less pleasant, you realize that scene 32, the highlight of the story, would have to vanish. It is no longer possible to retain scene 32, because it has some connection with scene 12. I understand that this present would not have been possible without that past. Life would have been something else, I don't know what. Since I like this life, I shouldn't complain. No one grows up without being emotionally hurt. I think it's impossible. I've had my share of hurt. From fifteen to twenty-five, the years that are supposed to be the prime of one's youth, life was very tough. In spite of that, there were great moments. Like, when I was eighteen, I was selected from Madhya Pradesh to represent Vikram University in a group discussion at a youth festival.

I had some wonderful friends. I wasn't a morose, withdrawn, sad child who pitied himself.

NMK: How did your father react to your ultimate success in films?

JA: Every father wants his son to become a very important person and he wishes him all the success. At the same time, don't forget that he's also a man, so he doesn't want the son to become greater than himself. Every son wants to look up to his father and wants to believe that his father is a great man. At the same time, he competes with his father and wants to outdo him. [smiles] I think it's a really paradoxical relationship, and I suppose my father felt these kinds of mixed emotions.

NMK: Was his real name Jaan Nisar Akhtar?

JA: Akhtar was his pen name like Majrooh is not Majrooh's real name, or Sahir is not his real name, or Kaifi. My father's takhallus, or what you call a pen name, was 'Akhtar' but it became part of his own name. It's something like 'Bachchan'—the pen name of Amitabh's father.

NMK: How old was your father when he died?

JA: He was sixty-two or sixty-three. Not very old. And I was thirty-one at the time. After he died, I discovered things about him that made me really think. My stepmother once told me that he'd often say, 'Remember one thing, I have another son and together we have other children, but the one who will look after you after I am dead and the one who will care about you is Javed.' Now, that's very strange because I did not believe I had given him any reason to think like that.

NMK: Did you ever discuss his poetry with him?

JA: Yes, and I'm quite sure that he was aware that I understood poetry. When I visited him in Bombay, quite often, he'd recite his latest poem or ghazal or whatever he had written. At many points, I objected to a line that I didn't like, then he'd argue with me. He once made a remark that left a deep impression on me. He said, 'It's very easy to write in difficult language, but it's very difficult to write in simple language—because you need tremendous command over language to put an intricate or complicated idea into simple words.' In my own writing, I tried to develop a diction that is simple, so it communicates and reaches people.

NMK: Do you think it's possible for someone to create a work that's genuinely original? Or is everything ultimately a reworking of what has been written or read before?

JA: It can be argued that there is no such thing as complete originality. The language we use is not original but learned from others. Most of the time, we are reproducing what

we've seen. But what's important is how we *use* information
or knowledge. We'd be making a mistake if we think that
information is an end in itself. Take food—it's not health, but
we need food to be healthy. But how does food give us health?
We eat and digest it and it turns into blood and energy in our
system. In the same way, if we read books or watch films,
they should run like blood in the veins of our imagination.
One could say in art we need four things: to observe, feel,
understand, and communicate what we have experienced.
Each and everyone of us is original. You see, there was never a
Nasreen Munni Kabir before and there will never be again. You
are at a position from where no one—but no one—has seen
this world before. And that's true of me, and of everyone else.
You are standing at a place—I am standing at a place—which
did not exist before. So I look at things from a perspective
that is totally new, and it would be wrong if I did not observe
something new. I should be able to see something that no
one else has seen. Logic dictates it. If I'm not seeing it, it
means I'm not seeing things from my point of view. Parroting
others is not good enough.

NMK: Do you think originality is synonymous with youth?

JA: It has nothing to do with youth. It has something to do
with your enthusiasm, your vulnerability, your curiosity and
your hunger to learn more. Look at Kurosawa—at the age of
eighty, the man made a film like *Dreams*. Well, some of us lose
it at the age of twenty-five. [*both laugh*]

NMK: It seems that every 20 years, a new energy is injected
into Hindi cinema. Take, for example, the 1930s, 1950s, and
1970s, we can identify key films in each of these decades that
were very important in the development of Hindi cinema—
films that have set the formula. Maybe it takes 20 years for new
movie directors—nourished on the cinema of a previous era—
to come into their own.

Take Guru Dutt—he was clearly influenced by the 1930s director P.C. Barua. So I believe this generation of filmmakers is influenced by the screenplays you and Salim Khan wrote.

JA: This is one interpretation. But it is a very interesting analysis and I think it holds.

NMK: The Salim-Javed scripts were most certainly at the heart of the 1970s.

What is the most important aspect of a script for you?

JA: It starts with the germ of an idea. It may be the plot, the characters, or a particular incident or twist. Sometimes you create a character and become fascinated by that character, and you weave a story around him or her. Sometimes you have the middle of the story, not the beginning or the end. But you have a twist in the plot.

In India, we still follow the Victorian script structure—because, even today, we have an interval in the middle of the film. So once you find an interesting interval point, you can roll the story back to the beginning, and then you can develop the second half of the story at a later point. Sometimes a one-line plot comes to you. In a finished script, the spine of the script is important. To some extent, you can afford to go wrong in a subplot, a scene, or a sequence but not in the basic structure of the story. Every story is some kind of parable, some kind of bridge. It starts from a point, and it should create some kind of symmetry that links incidents that are not apparently connected.

NMK: When you are credited with story, screenplay, and dialogue, what does this involve? I do not think the same division of labour applies to scripts written in Hollywood.

JA: You see, we had writers from Bengal and south India working in Hindi cinema. They understood the structure

of Hindi/Urdu cinema, but they didn't have a good enough
command over either language to be able to write the dialogue.
So they'd write the screenplay and a Hindi or Urdu writer
would then write the lines. That's how the different professions
of screenplay writer and dialogue writer became defined.

NMK: Can you tell me the difference between a story
and a screenplay? *Mr India*, for example, could essentially be
described as the story of a man who discovers a magic potion
that makes him invisible. This power enables him to combat
all evil forces.

JA: This is the outline of the story. The screenplay is what
happens to the character of *Mr India*—how to tell his story
onscreen. I'll give you an example. Suppose I tell you a
story of a man who is very poor—this is a very basic example,
not necessarily intended for you, but it is for people who are
unfamiliar with the term 'screenplay'. This impoverished
man goes hungry, but he does nothing that's dishonest. Now
this is the beginning of a story. How do I tell this story on the
screen? I can't use subtitles that read, 'Here goes an honest
man who is very poor.' So I *show* the man sleeping on the
pavement or living in a hut in a shantytown. One day, he passes
a restaurant and sees some people who are eating inside; he
looks at them through the glass window of the restaurant and
has a sad expression. We realize he's hungry. Suddenly a man
rushes past him and the man's wallet falls on the pavement.
Our hero picks up that wallet; it's full of currency notes. He
runs after the rich man and says, 'Sir, your wallet.' Our man
is unshaven and wearing dirty clothes. The rich man is taken
aback; he takes his wallet, looks at this poor fellow and tries
to give him 10 rupees or 100 rupees as a reward. Our hero
refuses to take the money; instead he says, 'I only did my
duty. I am a man of honour.' Now we realize here's a man
who is poor, hungry, honest, and also a man of principles.

So we understand everything about this man's character through incidents.

NMK: So is that the screenplay? And the dialogue is the exchange between the characters?

JA: Yes. When this honest man returns the wallet and the rich man offers him a reward, this exchange could be expressed in a hundred different ways. Now comes the turn of a good dialogue writer. What will the characters say in these circumstances? There is a beautiful line in a film written by Mr Inder Raj Anand. A poor man played by Raj Kapoor finds a wallet bulging with bank notes and returns it to its rich owner, who is played by Motilal. When Raj Kapoor gives the rich man his wallet, the rich man invites him to his home to attend a huge party full of even richer people.

NMK: Is the film *Anaari*?

JA: Yes, it is *Anaari*. This poor man comes to the party, but he's very intimidated and meekly asks, 'Who are these people?' His host answers with a cynical smile, 'Don't be intimidated by them…' 'Ye vo log hain jinhen tumhaari tarah sadakon pe noton se bhare batwe mile the, lekin unhone vapas nahin kiye' [These are people, who like you, happened to find a wallet stuffed with bank notes, but they never returned it].

NMK: Fabulous line! Now what about plots in Hindi films? Howard Hawks said there are about 30 plots in all of drama and the only new elements are the characters and how differently they do things.

How many basic plots do you think there are in the Indian context?

JA: I think 30 is too many, maybe 10. These are what you'd call master plots. Then there's the treatment, the characterization, and the minor incidents that make one story different from

another. Take a love story, now what's a love story? A boy and
girl fall in love, then they part because of some obstacle: they're
from different social classes, or they're of different religions, or
some adversary keeps them apart. In the end, they meet either
in life or in death. Ninety to ninety-nine per cent of love stories
depend on this plot—it's only the treatment that changes.
What's the difference between *Romeo and Juliet* and *Bobby*? It's
the same basic story.

NMK: But *Bobby* doesn't end in tragedy, the lovers live.

JA: That's a possible ending, and lovers can die. But then they
meet in death.

NMK: There has to be union.

JA: Union. Even in death.

NMK: Going back to basic film plots, what are these 10
plots? Are they inspired by the Hindu epics and Arabian story-
telling traditions?

JA: Roman mythology, Greek mythology, and Hindu
mythology. Classical stories. You find these plots in mythological
epics: the lost-and-found, the vendetta, the love story. The
lost-and-found is found in the story of *Rustom and Sohrab*. And
Shakuntala is also a lost-and-found story. You find the vendetta
story in mythology—somebody kills a child's parents, and the
child grows up and takes revenge. These master plots are inspired
from basic human instincts and so are made up of stories that
represent a particular human instinct or emotion: love, hate,
jealousy, curiosity, or whatever. So if your story relies heavily
on one particular instinct, the character will be obsessed with
love or hate.

NMK: People have often said that these master plots are based
on the nine rasas. I imagine this is close to your idea that basic
human instincts inspire plots. And because these instincts aren't

very numerous, repetition cannot be avoided. Maybe that's why
Indian popular cinema is always accused of being formulaic. So
how can a screenwriter innovate?

JA: The requirement of an Indian film writer is peculiar. He is
supposed to write a totally original script that has come before.
[*NMK laughs*]

NMK: Nothing too outrageously new?

JA: No. Mainstream Hollywood also has its dos and don'ts.
They too have their taboos: this will sell and this won't. But
perhaps they have a wider range than us.

We have many states in this country, all of them are Indian
states, but each has a different culture, tradition, and style. In
Gujarat, you have one kind of culture, then you go to Punjab, you
have another, and the same applies to Rajasthan, Bengal, Orissa,
or Kerala. There is one more state in this country, and that is Hindi
cinema. And so Hindi cinema also has its own culture. Punjabi
culture and Rajasthani culture may differ, but we understand the
differences—their cultures are not from different planets. In the
same way, Hindi cinema's culture is quite different from Indian
culture, but it's not alien to us, we understand it.

NMK: We understand all the codes.

JA: As a matter of fact, Hindi cinema is our closest
neighbour. It has its own world, its own traditions, symbols,
expressions, and its own language, and those who are familiar
with it, understand it. The nearest example for a non-Indian
to understand Hindi cinema is the Western. Never were there
sheriffs and gunslingers like the ones you see in a Western. And
never was there a small town with one street where a man starts
walking silently and waits for the other cowboy to draw his
gun. [*laughs*] The world of the Western has been developed by
Hollywood. And it has become a reality in itself.

NMK: It's the myth of the American past.

JA: It's a myth that Hollywood has created. In the same way, Hindi cinema has its own myths. It even has its own architecture: grand houses that have grand stairways leading to the living room!

NMK: A stairway to heaven!

JA: Yes! You see the father coming down these grand stairs wearing a dressing gown with a pipe in his hand. He stands on the steps and says pompously, 'Ye shaadi nahin ho sakti' [This marriage cannot take place]. Or you have a mother talking to the photograph of her dead husband, or a son telling his mother, 'Ma, mujhe samajhne ki koshish karo' [Mother, try and understand me]. I am quite convinced that in this country no son has ever said such a thing to his mother. In the 1930s, some writer must have translated 'Try and understand me' from the English.

NMK: It sounds like a line from a James Cagney film.

JA: It's a word-for-word translation of 'Try and understand me'.

NMK: When you think of Hollywood, who are your preferred directors in contemporary American cinema?

JA: Woody Allen and Steven Spielberg. I liked *Annie Hall*. This film looked at the fragility of human relationships in a neurotic society in an extremely humorous manner and without any sense of bitterness. To me, *Annie Hall* felt like a smile that hid a lot of sadness.

NMK: Which of Spielberg's films did you like?

JA: *E.T.*

NMK: Do you personally believe in extraterrestrial life?

JA: There are trillions of stars and galaxies in this large universe. To believe that life exists only on this planet and nowhere else is to believe that life is a miracle—and I don't believe in miracles. It does not mean that I believe in cigar-shaped UFOs that transport little green men either. [laughs] I don't think the vast distances involved would allow for any physical contact with other civilizations in the universe, but some day we may succeed in making some kind of radio contact. I think for the past 30 or 40 years, scientists and astronomers have been working in that direction. I'd give anything to see the day when they'd ultimately succeed.

NMK: Going back to the basic plots in Hindi films, how would you categorize classics like *Gunga Jumna* or *Deewaar*?

JA: With films like *Gunga Jumna* or *Deewaar*, you're on very safe ground. They may take on different garbs, they may display different furniture and settings, and different accents, but the films are based on classical plots. In our films too, we didn't experiment as far as the choice of plots was concerned. Classical plots have advantages and disadvantages: the advantage is that you're treading on safe ground, but the disadvantage is that you're walking on a much-trodden path. The crunch becomes, 'All right, you've taken a much-trodden path, but what kind of carpet are you going to lay down?'

NMK: People often talk about the influence of *Mother India* and *Gunga Jumna* on *Deewaar*. These three films clearly depend on classical plots. Do you think *Deewaar*'s comparison with these earlier classics is justified?

JA: In all honesty, yes. *Mother India* and *Gunga Jumna* were our favourite films, Salim Sahib's and mine. We really loved these pictures. They definitely influenced us. But I'll hasten to add that as we developed *Deewaar*'s script, it ceased to be either of these films. *Deewaar* resembled *Mother India* and *Gunga Jumna* in plot, but *Deewaar*'s sensibility was totally different. It was not only because the characters in the film wear western clothes, but the film's sensibility was very modern. We introduced a kind of modernity in the setting of the film, its accent, tempo, and language. *Deewaar's* cinematic language had also changed from the language of *Gunga Jumna*. It was more urban, more contemporary, and the kind of moral dilemmas that it posed were very much of its time.

NMK: The anger of the hero, Vijay, in *Deewaar* seems more internalized than the one expressed by Gunga in *Gunga Jumna*.

JA: Vijay's anger *was* internal. The film also poses questions that are more universal than the questions raised in *Gunga Jumna*. For example, whatever was happening was happening to Gunga alone. In *Deewaar*, what was happening to Vijay was happening to many of us. Maybe we did not react like Vijay, but we could identify with him more than we could with Gunga.

NMK: If Gunga's anger is a reaction to the injustice inflicted on him and his mother and on his love, Dhanno, Vijay's anger is also a reaction to the injustice that he saw inflicted on his father.

JA: And on his mother and the dockworkers.

NMK: Is Vijay's anger rooted in revenge?

JA: No, he never goes in search of the man who made his father suffer. He never goes after the munshi [manager] who misbehaved with his mother. Vijay knows it is the system that is the exploiter. He sees the same exploitation at work at the docks. He revolts when he sees a dockworker dying at the hands of thugs and when he sees that the dockworkers are obliged to pay protection money—that is when Vijay revolts.

NMK: Vijay is also filled with rage. It seems that he cannot forgive himself for not being able to save his mother or his father from the terrible shame and humiliation they have suffered for no fault of their own.

JA: I feel that on some level Vijay is also angry with his father, who accepted defeat and who could not stand up and fight. In a later scene in *Deewaar*, Vijay's mother tells him, 'Why didn't you walk away from the fight?' And Vijay answers, 'Are you suggesting that I too should have run away?' Now this 'too' is very important. His mother then slaps Vijay. He is angry with life because it has created a terrible situation for his father. Vijay is not very happy with the world.

NMK: Vijay can easily fight in the world of men, but what is his relationship to the world of women?

JA: Heroes like Vijay have nothing against women. They have great respect for women. But they are too shy, too introverted to show their emotions, or even accept their emotions. The only way that people who have been hurt very badly protect themselves is by hiding their emotions. If they showed them, it would hurt even more. So they develop a kind of hard crust, although they are soft and vulnerable people behind that hard crust.

NMK: How would you describe Vijay's relationship with the women in his life?

JA: Vijay's relationship with the character played by Parveen Babi in *Deewaar*, or his relationship with the character Raakhee played in *Trishul* is similar—it is very difficult for Vijay to tell these women that he loves them. It is equally difficult for him to express his love for his brother or for his mother. There is a storm raging within him so he has closed the doors. That is how such characters feel safe. They create a deewaar [wall] between themselves and their emotions.

NMK: That's very interesting. One always imagined the title of the film referred to the wall between good and bad and not a wall to hold emotions in.

JA: You have to keep guessing. The only time Vijay breaks down to a certain extent is in the temple in the final scene of the film.

NMK: But even then, he is not expressing his feelings to a fellow human being but to god. On another point, *Deewaar* was perhaps one of the first Hindi films in which the extended family is hugely reduced within the narrative. Various family members, usually seen on the Hindi screen, end up here being represented solely by one parent. I think you and Salim Sahib started this trend of reducing the screen family to a single character—that of the mother.

JA: We were not conscious of it. What's for sure is that the mother was always a respected figure in Hindi cinema, but *Deewaar* gave the mother central importance. *Deewaar* turned the mother figure into a symbol of a certain value system, a symbol of purity, and a link between the modern and the past and tradition.

NMK: When *Deewaar* was released, did you see it in a cinema hall?

JA: Oh yes, I did.

NMK: How did the audience react?

JA: There was a tremendous reaction. I also remember how people reacted to *Zanjeer*. It was the first film of its kind. The reaction was very unusual. People did not clap or whistle in the theatre; they watched the film in total silence and awe. I saw *Zanjeer* in different theatres, perhaps seven times in all. I was once watching the film in Gaiety Cinema, or it could have been Galaxy, in Bandra. I remember somebody was sitting behind me, and in the scene in which Amitabh loses his temper at the police station in front of Pran—I could hear awe in the man's voice when he said, 'Arre, baap re baap' [Oh my god]! Now this is something I had never heard before, and have never heard since. So by the time the audience saw *Deewaar,* they were already familiar with that kind of anger. In *Zanjeer*, it was a totally new experience for them.

NMK: Vijay, the hero of *Zanjeer* played by Amitabh Bachchan, was a very different kind of hero.

JA: It's not a surprise that so many actors who were offered the lead role in *Zanjeer* did not take it. Because they couldn't understand the kind of a hero that Vijay was. Was he a hero at all?

NMK: Who were the other actors considered for the part?

JA: Dharamji [Dharmendra] was supposed to do the film. Dev Sahib [Dev Anand] heard the script, so did Raaj Kumar and some other actors too. [The script is usually narrated to actors rather than read by an actor.]

NMK: I am sure the actors who heard your scripts must have been struck by their difference. I'm curious to know whether you favoured naturalism in your writing—naturalism in Indian film dialogue does not seem to be of high priority.

JA: I don't know. Literature had influenced me, and like many other people, I had a weakness for a good line. But at the same time, I'll say that I was influenced to some extent by the modern American novel. Not great literature, to be honest, but bestsellers, paperbacks. They taught me one thing: precision. One-liners. Saying things in a few words, making an art of the understatement—saying less than you want to and leaving the rest to the imagination. Exaggeration is supposed to show command over language in India. Perhaps it relates to conventions in social communication. Exaggeration is even traditionally accepted in literature. In theatre and cinema, we nearly always had lengthy dialogue, full of similes, metaphors, and an overdose of melodrama. Every time a film character would try to describe his emotions, he'd launch into a great speech. We did not do that. Our dialogue was intense but usually crisp, despite the fact that one of *Sholay*'s characters, Gabbar, for example, indulges in long soliloquies, but his lines are short. The audience not only enjoyed our dialogue but could also fill in the gaps. None of our heroes ever told his beloved that he loved her or that he had even fallen in love. In none of the films do our characters tell the villain that they hate him. There is never a direct expression of any emotion; emotions are hinted at; they are suggested. So this style of dialogue is like a long chain of iceberg tips, and the icebergs are left to your imagination.

NMK: In that way, the audience is encouraged to participate in the dialogue through their imagination. Many Hindi films tend to be quite obvious and also quite theatrical: did you try to avoid being theatrical?

JA: We never indulged in rhetoric. What we realized is that if you want to give highs, you must give lows. So if you see our pictures, the dialogue is not hugely theatrical or dramatic. But it cleverly makes proper bridges. It slips in and out of a theatrical mould. Because the transition between naturalism and a theatrical tone is slow and smooth in our films, the theatrical moments seem convincing. Indian dialogue writers make the fatal mistake of trying to turn every line into a punchline. That creates a sense of numbness in the viewer, so when the real punchline is finally spoken, it does not stand out. We never did that. We never tried to be very clever with the dialogue. Only at the right moment would we strike, otherwise we played the drama in a very low key.

NMK: Everyone talks about the scene in *Deewaar* in which Ravi says, 'Mere paas Ma hai' [I have Mother]. That's a good example of an effective and understated punchline.

JA: Ravi could have said all kinds of things, like, 'Aaj mere paas Ma ka pyaar hai, mujhe ye mil gaya, mujhe vo mil gaya ...' [Today I have my mother's love, I have this, I have that ...]. In contrast, take Vijay, the other character in the scene, who is providing the platform for this punchline. He has many lines before Ravi makes his mark with this single statement, and it works. Perhaps Ravi's punchline would not have worked quite as well without Vijay's extended dialogue that preceded it. You have to orchestrate a scene. If you try to bombard the listener's sensibility all the time, his sensibility will be so battered that when you want him to feel something, he'll be too exhausted.

NMK: When I look at Hindi film posters of the 1970s, it seems that you and Salim Khan were the first writers whose names appeared on posters.

JA: No, we weren't the first. Pandit Mukhram Sharma's name figured on film posters. I was in college or school, when *Dhool ka Phool* was released. A very big banner, B.R. Films, produced the movie, and the publicity material read, 'Pandit Mukhram Sharma's *Dhool ka Phool*'.

NMK: Was that unusual for the time?

JA: That was unusual. I think only Pandit Mukhram Sharma had acquired that position. But after that, the next time it happened was with us. We made films with different directors, but I think the audiences could spot the same sensibility at work. So besides the inclusion of Amitabh in the cast list, we were the common factor in many films. For example, Yash Chopra directed *Trishul* and *Deewaar*; *Zanjeer* was directed by Prakash Mehra, and Ramesh Sippy directed *Shakti*; and yet you can see a common sensibility and an emotional intensity that links them. You can recognize our signature.

NMK: Yes, these films clearly had the Salim-Javed stamp.

I am wondering, when did you come to Bombay? And was it to work in films?

JA: I came in the first week of September 1964.

NMK: Was it in September or October? I read somewhere you came to Bombay to meet Guru Dutt, but didn't meet him because five days later he had committed suicide. If the article had quoted you correctly, then you would have arrived here in October, not September—because Guru Dutt died on 10 October 1964.

JA: 10 October? Then I stand corrected. I came to Bombay on 4 October 1964. I worked as a clapper boy for producer-director Kamal Amrohi for a salary of 50 rupees a month. After a while, in 1965, I got a job with the director S.M. Sagar. I worked with him as an assistant and a clapper boy on his 1966 film *Sarhadi Lutera*. He was making a stunt film with the actor Sheikh Mukhtar and Salim Sahib was acting in a romantic role. S.M. Sagar could not find a dialogue writer, so I was asked if I would write a few scenes. S.M. Sagar liked my writing and said, 'You write the dialogue.' So besides being the clapper boy, I became the dialogue writer as well. That's where I met Salim Sahib.

NMK: Was it during that time that Salim Khan gave up acting?

JA: Not at that point, but ultimately he gave it up. Even at that time, he used to think up stories. After S.M. Sagar's film was made, we kept in touch. In 1968, I was living in Andheri; then I moved to Bandra and got a little place to live, which was not very far from Salim Sahib's house. In the evenings, I'd go to his place if I had nothing to do. That's how our friendship grew. We'd sit together and make up stories. In the intervening years, he sold the story of *Do Bhai* to the director Brij. The film had Ashok Kumar, Jeetendra, and Mala Sinha—it was Salim Sahib's story. The film didn't do well, but that doesn't matter. I wrote the dialogue for a film called *Yakeen*, and that didn't do well either. These films didn't help us as writers. So we were both without work. As luck would have it, S.M. Sagar met us again. He knew Salim Sahib and I could write and said, 'I have a short story. I'll give you some money to develop it into a screenplay.' Salim Sahib and I agreed and started working together on that particular film, and so we wrote the screenplay of *Adhikar*. The film had Ashok Kumar and Nanda— our names did not even feature in the credits.

NMK: How did you both get established as screenwriters?

JA: Sudhir Wahi, S.M. Sagar's assistant, had heard our screenplay of *Adhikar* and liked it. He knew Narendra Bedi at Sippy Films and he told us, 'Why don't you go to Sippy Films? They're setting up a story department and they're looking for new writers.' So we went to Sippy Films, and Salim Sahib and I found ourselves working together again. That's where we met Rajesh Khanna. He heard a script that we had written and liked it very much. One day, Rajesh Khanna called us and asked, 'Why don't you write a screenplay for me? I have signed a picture in the south—it's about some elephant and a man [reference to *Haathi mere Saathi*]. It's a very odd story, but I can't walk out of the picture because the producer has paid me a very large signing amount. And I have to buy a house, so I must do this film. But can you do something about this atrocious script? I'll talk to the producer to pay you and to give you credit.' Salim Sahib and I had not intended to become partners—it just happened.

NMK: Isn't it quite difficult to write a script in tandem?

JA: Why? In Hollywood, three or four writers work on a script together.

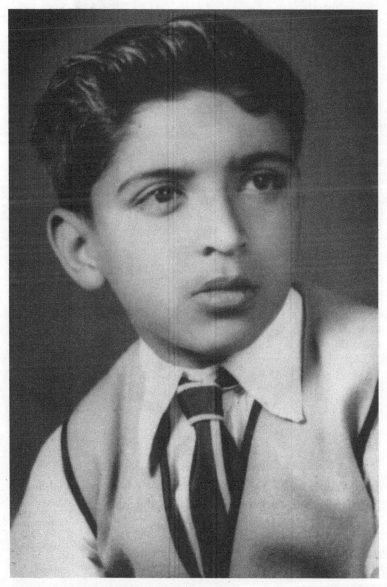

Javed Akhtar, aged 14. Photographed in an art studio in Aligarh owned by Banwari Lal, 1957.

Javed Akhtar, aged 11, in his grandfather's house, 'Dar-ul-Siraj', New Hyderabad, Lucknow. Photograph: Abu Salim.

Safia Akhtar and her two sons, Javed (aged 5) and Salman (aged 3½), in a photographer's studio in Nainital, 1950.

Jaan Nisar Akhtar and his two sons, Javed and Salman, Lucknow, 1957. Photograph: Abu Salim.

Bombay, 1977. Photograph: Gautam Rajadhyaksha.

With his wife, Shabana Azmi, on the sets of Mrinal Sen's film
Ek Din Achanak.

With Amitabh and Jaya Bachchan at Faiz Ahmed Faiz's poetry recital held at Akhtar's home in Bandra, Bombay, 1979. Photograph: Sanil.

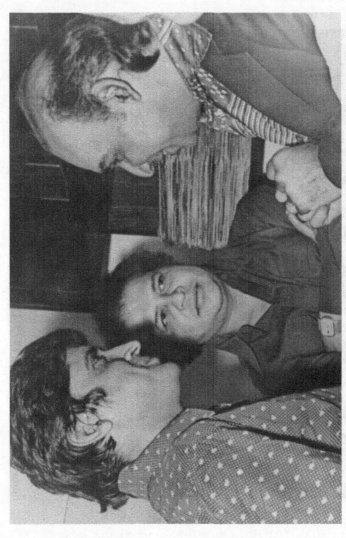

With music composer Laxmikant (middle) and Yash Chopra at Akhtar's home, 1978. Photograph: Sanil.

NMK: What do you think was the most positive thing about two writers working together on a script?

JA: [*long pause*] Oh, we were a great team! There was no doubt about it. We really complemented each other for a very long time. He had everything that I didn't have, and I had everything he didn't have. As a writer, he had the courage and I had the intricacy. He brought to our work broad and bold strokes of drama, and I had the detail and the finesse. It was a deadly combination!

NMK: What kind of boldness did Salim Khan have?

JA: How do I define it? It's the power in drama, the boldness in developing the story. Bringing something extraneous to the script, thinking of something new. Boom! Oh yes! This situation can happen too—something that would shock. He had that in him. I had a very good understanding of characterization and the finer details. Salim Sahib had come to films with a very new, fresh, and dynamic understanding of a screenplay. His school was basically the Hollywood movies of the 1940s and 1950s. He talked about films like *The Big Country*, melodramas like *Written on the Wind*, romantic films, and films with a big canvas. He had a new understanding of screenplay writing, and I must say, in all honesty, that I learned a lot about screenplays from him.

NMK: When you say screenplays, you mean how to build incidents?

JA: Yes, and the tempo. The structure. Sometimes I think he might have been slightly rough in approach—in particular scenes. But he'd bring very strong and potent situations and material to a screenplay. Maybe that's why we were a good combination.

NMK: How did the two of you divide the work?

JA: This is a question we've always avoided answering. As a team, we gave in a complete script, a finished product. We never went into details about who did what and how. To now say, 'this was mine and that was his'—talking about it after so many years is not the right thing to do.

NMK: People often say that in India the script and dialogue are written at the last minute. Was that true of the way the two of you worked?

JA: No. It may have happened and I hear it still does, but never with us. We always gave in complete scripts. In the beginning we were known to be rather stubborn and averse to making any changes in the script. It wasn't that we were not flexible—but you see we had to fight a system in which a script was not at all important. Scripts were developed according to the whims and fancies of the director, the actor, the actress, or the producer. So we fought against that practice, and that gave us a bad name and a good name. We created many enemies in the process because we stepped on many toes, but those feet shouldn't have come in the way in the first place. Agreed? [both laugh]

NMK: In America, the director often fights over the final cut with the producer. Did you, as writers, have any say in the final cut?

JA: The system in India has not defined such things. It is a matter of who calls the shots in each situation. The final cut depends on the power of many, including the producer, the financier, the leading man, or the director. A powerful distributor can also insist that you add a qawwali [devotional song] here or a cabaret there. In our case, sometimes we called the shots.

NMK: When you were writing scripts, did you also provide shot divisions?

JA: Yes. Even now when I write, I write a scene in minute detail. But the scenes in the script are broad guidelines for a director. Ultimately, it is the director's prerogative to shoot it in the way he wants. But obviously our descriptions used to be of great help. Sometimes the director would follow our shot divisions, and sometimes he would not.

NMK: At least you offered a complete concept of a scene. When you write, do you write in Hindi or Urdu?

JA: I write the dialogue in Urdu, but the action and descriptions are in English. Then an assistant transcribes the Urdu script into Devanagari because most people read Hindi, not Urdu. I write in Urdu. It's not just me; I think most writers working in this so-called Hindi cinema write in Urdu, including Gulzar, Rajinder Singh Bedi, Inder Raj Anand, Rahi Masoom Raza, and Vahajat Mirza, who wrote the screenplay and dialogue for films like *Mughal-e-Azam*, *Gunga Jumna*, and *Mother India*. So most dialogue writers and most songwriters were from the Urdu tradition.

NMK: How did this come about?

JA: The relationship between show business and Urdu goes back to a time before the first talkie, *Alam Ara*, which was made in 1931. Before that you had the popular urban theatre known as the Urdu Parsee Theatre. It got its name because, by and large, these theatres were owned and run by Bombay Parsees. The early stage productions were adaptations of Shakespearean and Victorian plays, and these plays were presented in a certain style: they had drama and comedy, and included many songs. A play could be about Marcus and Helena and set in Rome, but when Helena would pine for love, she would sing, 'Pia more aaj nahin aaye' [My beloved has not come to me today].

Then followed the writing of original plays—and these were mostly written by Urdu writers like Agha Hashr Kashmiri or Munshi Bedil. They were exceptionally good plays. And so the Indian talkie inherited its basic structure from the Urdu Parsee Theatre, and that's how the sound films started with Urdu. Even New Theatres in Calcutta [Kolkata] used Urdu writers. You see, Urdu was the lingua franca of urban northern India before the Partition, and it was the language understood by most people. And it was—and still is—an extremely sophisticated language capable of portraying all kinds of emotions and drama.

NMK: Were those involved with this theatre really Parsees?

JA: Yes. For example, Sohrab Modi was of the Parsee community. He made the film *Yahudi*, which was based on a play by Agha Hashr Kashmiri called *Yahudi ki Ladki*, which was written for the stage. Most of the film's dialogue was taken from that play, including the lines: 'Tumhaara khoon khoon hai, hamaara khoon paani' [Your blood is blood. My blood is water]. Some of Kashmiri Sahib's theatre dialogue was written in rhyme. I don't think that he wrote for cinema—I believe he died soon after the Indian sound films were made. But films have used a lot of his material.

I have many of his plays that were published in the 1920s and 1930s. I'll read you a scene from 'Aseer-e-Hirs' [The Prisoner of Greed]. The story is about Changez Khan who is in love with a girl called Naushaba.

CHANGEZ: Khair ye to farmaaiye, vo tohfa mera qabool hua, matlab vasool hua?
[Pray tell me, did you accept the gift that I have sent you? Did you guess its meaning?]
NAUSHABA: Saboot shukar ka zaahir meri zabaan se hai, tumhaara tohfa to mujhko qabool jaan se hai. Magar pyaar se ek sawaal hai.
[The proof of gratitude comes from my words. My very life accepts your gift—but I have a question for Love.]

CHANGEZ: Farmaaiye vo kya khayaal hai?

[Pray, what is that thought?]

NAUSHABA: Kumhaar jo mitti ka khilona banaata hai, vo kis kaam aata hai?

[The clay toy a potter makes—what use is it?]

CHANGEZ: Usse dil behelaaya jaata hai. Agar vo kisi ke haath se chhoot jaaye, ya thokar se toot jaaye, to kumhaar ko sakht malaal hoga.

[It is to amuse a heart. But if it slips through one's fingers, or is shattered, the potter will be deeply dejected.]

NAUSHABA: Kyon aisa khayaal hoga?

[Why would he feel so?]

CHANGEZ: Kyon ki us shakhs ne kumhaar ki mehnat barbaad kar di.

[Because that person has spoilt the potter's efforts.]

NAUSHABA: Vah, subhaanallah. Khoob baat irshaad kar di.

[Glory be to Allah. Well spoken!]

NMK: Fantastic lines! They remind me of *Cyrano de Bergerac*. Tell me, when you write, do you need the contact of people, or do you prefer writing when you're alone?

JA: Ultimately, you write alone. Writing is a lonely job, but I suppose it is necessary for a writer to have contact with life. If you start living in isolation, or in a very small circle, you lose touch. How long can you depend on your memory for a new expression, new characters, or styles of conversation, or metaphors and similes? If you're a writer, and that's your job, you pick things up unconsciously when you meet people and talk to them. And one day they come in handy.

NMK: I went to a writers' discussion panel recently in London, and Richard Curtis, who wrote the popular British film, *Four Weddings and a Funeral*, said that when he finished a script, he'd take a character's lines and speak in his or her voice for an entire day. And then he'd do the same with the dialogue of each character, and in this way, he'd test whether his dialogue 'sounded' real. Did you have a technique to hear the voice of your characters?

JA: In the first scene, your characters are stranger to you. You try to understand them. In the second scene, you might understand the style of the character, and come to know the character. Whether it's Basanti, Gabbar, Vijay, Mogambo, or Arjun—you try to understand his or her psychology. When you listen to people, you should notice the particular style they have of speaking, what stress they place on different words. You remember such phrases and expressions, and how a person constructs a sentence. Then your character's expression is more or less a composite of the different people that you have met.

NMK: The names of Hindi film characters are very important because names provide the audience with information relating to the social status and religion of the character. Names like Amar or Akbar immediately tell the audience that Amar is Hindu and Akbar is Muslim. If a Hindu character is called Sharma, you know the character is a brahmin. Was the naming of your characters important?

JA: You can easily distinguish between a Hindu or a Muslim character. That's very easy. But certain names have certain associations, they create certain images or references in your subconscious, and that's important too. Phonetic sounds like the names Daaga or Tejaa, these sounds are interesting in themselves. Davar gives you a sense of power. This sound, 'Davar', has no fibres dangling from it at all. It has crispness. It starts and ends in a definite manner. Davar's name could have easily been Bhikulaal—but it would not have suited that character in *Deewaar*.

So you have to think of names that will create an image or have an effect that you want to evoke in the viewer's subconscious.

That's important. As far as the question of where the character was born, as I said, Hindi cinema is another state within India, so we never needed to identify the specific region he or she comes from.

NMK: Someone from the Hindi-speaking belt?

JA: Yes. He's usually an upper-class or middle-class person. If the hero is poor and he lives in Bombay, then he's probably from UP.

NMK: Or from Bihar?

JA: UP, not Bihar.

NMK: Is it because of the difference in language?

JA: Yes, his language would be different if he were from Bihar. Most Hindi cinema characters are based on a Delhi, Haryana, or UP model but they have an 'all-India' culture. So a female character can be seen dancing a typical Punjabi bhangra, and in another scene, she can be seen performing a south Indian dance like Bharat Natyam. So we pick and choose different cultural aspects from different regions and mix them together.

NMK: So the Hindi film hero is a kind of a composite character?

JA: He's from everywhere and from nowhere.

NMK: When I hear you describe the names of your characters, I wonder whether you are influenced by the sound a word evokes . . .

JA: Maybe I am. But I'm not consciously aware of it. In language, phonetics has great importance. Phonetics is the physical appearance of language. Take the name Davar again. Davar is an Indian name. Because it starts with 'd' and ends with 'r', it has a certain ring of Western sophistication. The sound 'd' is often the first sound of a Western name: Don, Donald, or David. You won't find many names in India that start with 'd' and end on 'r'.

So crisp. It's possible that a villager may be called Davar. But I wouldn't give a villager such a name, neither would I name a paan-eating man 'Davar'. But it can happen—you could meet a villager called Davar. If you go to the Punjab, you'll meet men who are six-foot-three and have broken noses because they were boxers in their college days, and they are called Pinky. [*both laugh*]

NMK: How many versions or drafts of a script would you write before you and Salim Khan were satisfied? Five, or six?

JA: Only one version. Never a second.

NMK: Never? You mean your scripts were written in one go? That's extraordinary. People write and rewrite so many drafts.

JA: *Deewaar* was written in one go, *Zanjeer* was in one go, *Sholay* as well. *Haath ki Safai, Akhri Daur, Majboor*, and *Yaadon ki Baraat*—these scripts were all written in one go, both dialogue and screenplay. All the pictures that matter in our writing career—and are still talked about—were based on scripts written in one go. The first time that we revised a script was for our fourteenth or fifteenth film: *Trishul*. And the scene that was revised was written after the picture was shot. When we saw the first cut of *Trishul*, we did not like the second half, so some scenes post-interval were re-shot.

NMK: How long did it take you both to write a script?

JA: In the case of *Deewaar*'s screenplay—the detailed screenplay minus the dialogue—was written in eighteen days.

NMK: Eighteen days?

JA: Exactly eighteen days. I remember that.

NMK: So it just flowed out?

JA: That was the time when we were really brimming with ideas and energy. The dialogue must have taken us about twenty-five days. Dialogue writing is a tedious job, you have to write every line!

NMK: As you gained more and more experience in scriptwriting, could you start predicting how the audience would react to certain scenes?

JA: Everybody predicts reactions to their work, whether you're a public orator, a performer, singer, or dancer. Sometimes you get a reaction you're not expecting—an element in a film that becomes very popular. The director Shekhar Kapur gave us an example in a recent interview. When the final cut of *Mr India* was ready, Shekhar felt that the line 'Mogambo khush hua' [Mogambo is pleased] was repeated too often in the film. So he cut it from a few scenes, and I told him not to cut that line from any scene. I was quite convinced that this line was going to become a kind of a buzz line. I told Shekhar that if the film would run at all, everybody in the country would repeat Mogambo's catchphrase. And that's what eventually happened.

NMK: This sort of 'quotable quote' is less common in Hollywood, though of course you have the famous line from *The Godfather*…

JA [*instantly*]: '…make him an offer he can't refuse.'

NMK: As far as I can tell, American cinema does not provide as many quotable quotes as Hindi cinema. Vast numbers of people remember Hindi dialogue and can quote line after line with great ease. Why do you think that is?

JA: I think we give a lot of importance to the spoken word. Our cinema is still heavily influenced by traditional theatre, and so cinema relies heavily on the spoken word. For us, it is an audiovisual medium and the 'a' is very, very capital. Audiovisual! [*NMK laughs*]

NMK: Was *Sholay* inspired by any book or movie? For example, Kurosawa's *Seven Samurai*?

JA: No. More by films like *The Magnificent Seven* and *The Five Man Army*. I don't remember if *The Five Man Army* was released before *Sholay*, but *The Magnificent Seven* had been released. The concept of mercenaries had definitely come to us from Western cinema. That's true. But the whole plot, the story, is not taken from anywhere else.

NMK: Wasn't there a 1956 film that had the same title '*Shole*'?

JA: It was made by B.R. Chopra, and perhaps it was his first film. I was a kid when I saw it. Remember they spelt the title as '*Shole*'? I never liked that spelling because it is so weak. But if you spell the word as '*Sholay*'—it evokes a vista, a sense of grandeur.

NMK: In the West, some film critics called *Sholay* a 'curry' Western. Did that amuse you?

JA: [*smiling*] There's some truth in it. I must accept, there's some truth in it. There was a director—what's his name—the man who made *A Fistful of Dollars*?

NMK: Sergio Leone.

JA: Sergio Leone. We were very influenced by him. I would say that there is some Mexican blood in Gabbar. He's a bandit, not a daaku [dacoit]. So Leone's influences are there. Like in the massacre scene where Thakur comes home to see the dead bodies of his whole family lying on the ground—there was such a scene in *Once Upon a Time in the West*. We were very impressed by it, and we wrote a similar scene. But, by and large, most of the script and characters in *Sholay* were totally original, and were created by us. I can't think of any other Hindi film that has five or six characters that are equally well known as Gabbar, Surma Bhopali, Basanti, Jai and Veeru, and Jailer. These characters are known even today years after the film was released in 1975. These characters appear in adverts, in comedy sitcoms. Even Sambha does!

When I was writing Gabbar Singh's first scene, I wanted to say that there is a reward of 50,000 rupees on his head—50,000 was obviously a big amount in the 1970s. At that point, there was no character in the script called Sambha. When I was writing it, I thought it was below Gabbar's dignity to have to say, 'I have a 50,000 rupees reward on my head.' A man with his kind of arrogance and conceit would more likely ask a subordinate—or rather order him—to boast his worth. That's why I wrote:

> GABBAR: Arre o Sambha, kitna inaam rakkhe hain sarkaar hum par?
> SAMBHA: Poore pachaas hazaar.
> GABBAR: Suna? Poore pachaas hazaar.
> [GABBAR: Sambha! How much reward has the government put on my head?
> SAMBHA: Full fifty thousand.
> GABBAR: Hear that? Full fifty thousand!]

Gabbar does not say it himself. Now after finishing the scene, I realized this was an interesting narrative device. So in the next scene involving Gabbar, I used the same technique—Sambha mirrors or echoes what Gabbar will not say himself—and it became a particular style.

I thoroughly enjoyed the experience of *Sholay*. In my whole career, Gabbar Singh was one of the few characters that I enjoyed writing—because Gabbar was developing his own vocabulary. I remember very clearly that while writing *Sholay*, I would get very excited and relish the prospect that once I completed a few scenes, the next would have Gabbar in it. Let's see what he will say now.

NMK: He came alive for you?

JA: He came alive for me. There are so many words in
Gabbar's vocabulary that I was not even aware of. I didn't know
for sure if I could use those words. Take Gabbar's dialogue

Arre o Sambha! Ye Ramgarhwaale apni betiyon ko kaun chakki
ka pisa aata khilaate hain re? Haath paaon to dekh daari ke, bahut
karaare hain saale, bahut karaare.
[O Sambha! I wonder what kind of wheat the people of Ramgarh
feed their daughters. Just look, how sturdy her limbs are!]

Now karaare [sturdiness] is a word I would personally never use
for a woman's limbs.

Aur kachehri mein aisa taap mujh ko, aisa taap mujh ko...
[In the courthouse, I felt my temperature rise/my blood boil...]

Gabbar could have said instead, 'aisa ghussa aaya mujh ko' [I
was enraged]. 'Taap' is a strange word. As a matter of fact, it
is not the right word to express anger. 'Taap' actually means
'fever'. Instinctively, I knew this is what he would say. I would
never write such lines for any other character. Gabbar had his
own language. The sadism is in his choice of words: 'khurach-
khurach' [scratch away]—there's nothing smooth about it.
There is a strange kind of cruelty and coarseness in his way
of speaking: 'Dekho chhamiya, zyaada nakhre mat karo hum
se, nahin to ye gori chamdi hai na—saare badan se khurach-
khurach ke utaar doonga' [Look, girl, don't get too coy with
me, or I'll scratch away the fair skin off your whole body].
His aesthetics are so low that he doesn't think such words
are crude.

It's not the end but the process that gives him pleasure. When
he looks at Thakur who is fighting for his life, the usual dialogue
would be, 'Dekho kaisa jhatke maar raha hai, kaisa lad raha
hai. Kaisa haatha-paaye kar raha hai' [See how he twitches. See

how he resists. See him crashing his legs and arms about]. But Gabbar uses a word to describe Thakur's movements that is often used for the movement of birds. And a bird only reacts like that if it is dying. [*JA, increasingly excited*] 'Kaise phad-phada raha hai saala' [See the bastard's limbs flap about].

In another scene, Gabbar looks full of concern for Kaalia's plight; but Kaalia's sole judge and executioner is Gabbar himself. He says, 'Ab tera kya hoga, Kaalia?' [What will become of you, Kaalia?]

Gabbar is a strange man. Showing concern when he is the master of Kaalia's fate. Will he kill him? Will he spare him? Who knows!

The dialogue was written in such a way that you should never be able to guess whether it will lead to a high or a low dramatic point. There are eight or nine scenes in which Gabbar appears, but in each of these scenes, you're on edge, guessing his next move. There is an inherent unpredictability in Gabbar's character, not only in his actions but in his way of speaking too: 'Kitne aadmi the? Vo do aur tum teen, phir bhi waapas aa gaye?' [How many men were there? Only two? And yet you came back?]

Now you think Gabbar will lose his temper, but he doesn't— he says, 'Kya samajh kar aaye? Ki sardar bahut khush hoga?' [What did you think? That your master would be very pleased?]

Then he shouts out, 'Dhitkaar hai!' [Shame on you!] So you think he's going to keep shouting from then on. He doesn't, and suddenly his pitch falls again. You're fascinated by Gabbar's unpredictability because it instils a kind of fear that leaves you guessing.

NMK: That's far more unnerving.

JA: Unnerving. And that grips you too. It's like going for a—what do you call that?

NMK: A rollercoaster ride?

JA: Oh, my God, will it go down? No, it goes up. Gabbar's personality is like that.

NMK: Gabbar is also taunting and boastful, and capable of uncontrollable rage. When Gabbar escapes prison and is on a rampage of revenge, he tells Thakur with great delight, 'Phanda khul gaya' [the noose has come untied]. But this statement can also be seen as freeing Thakur from his own sense of right and wrong. When Thakur sees his family annihilated by Gabbar, he becomes as lawless as Gabbar and takes revenge outside the law. Thakur is the kind of person who crosses the line when faced with injustice.

I suppose one can say that despite its large canvas, at the heart of *Sholay* is the story of two vengeful men: Gabbar and Thakur.

JA: But Gabbar deprived Thakur of his two hands—and that was his justification for revenge. And so, ultimately, Jai and Veeru enter the narrative and become Thakur's two hands.

NMK: Hired hands.

JA: As you say, the story is centred on Gabbar and Thakur and the war between them. If you look at these characters, you see they are opposites. Gabbar is dirty, unshaven, verbose. Thakur barely speaks—he is very clean, dignified, poised, while Gabbar is boastful, boisterous. Thakur always underplays a situation. They are dramatically different from each other. The reference to the dialogue 'Phanda khul gaya' [the noose has come untied] is actually from the scene in which Thakur is riding a horse and chases Gabbar. Gabbar tries to run away from him, but Thakur grabs him by the neck. He uses his arms around Gabbar's neck like a noose and says, 'Ye haath nahin, phansi ka phanda hai, Gabbar' [These are not hands, they are a hangman's noose, Gabbar].

So Thakur's hands, his arms, preyed on Gabbar's mind. The hands that held the reins of the horse that tracked him down, the hands that grabbed him by the neck. So Gabbar hated those hands—those arms of the law.

NMK: But Gabbar seeks a most terrible revenge by cutting off Thakur's arms. In the West, a comparable revenge would be castration, yet in *Mother India* and in *Sholay*, the heroes aren't castrated but lose both arms. These are powerful symbols—is it because hands and arms denote a man's role as protector and provider?

JA: You see, you become less of a man if you have lost your arms. Hands make us human. Hands allow you to participate, otherwise you are just a witness. When Thakur spits on Gabbar's face, he warns Thakur, 'Thook le Thakur, lekin vo haal kar ke chodunga tera ki duniya thookegi tujh par' [Spit on me if you want, Thakur, but one day I will leave you in such a condition that the world will spit on you]. Gabbar wants to give Thakur a life that is worse than death.

NMK: In Indian cinema, having no arms is like a life sentence, the severest imprisonment. No less than being locked away for life as Gabbar was supposed to be.

Had you always imagined Amjad Khan in the role of Gabbar?

JA: Not at all. Not at all.

NMK: Had you imagined another actor?

JA: When the script was being written, we had no actor in our minds. When the dialogue was completed, I remember there were two actors who were cast in *Sholay* who wanted Gabbar's part. One was Sanjeev Kumar who said, 'I'd like to play Gabbar.' And the other was Amitabh. He said, 'If you give me Gabbar, I'd be very happy.' He wanted the villain's role. We did not have many actors to choose from.

Danny Denzongpa was originally signed, but one was not too excited. Danny was a successful villain, but he had some date problems. So he opted out because he had some other film to shoot. We were left with no alternatives. And then we suggested Amjad Khan.

NMK: Where had you seen him perform?

JA: I had seen him in 1963 in Delhi when I had gone for a youth festival. Amjad and his brother Imtiaz had come from Bombay University with a play called 'Ae mere watan ke logon' [O People of My Country]. It was about the Chinese invasion. Amjad played an army officer, and he was brilliant. The play left a deep impression on me, and I had mentioned him quite a few times to Salim Sahib. So when we were short of suggestions for actors, Salim Sahib said, 'You've always said that Amjad is a very fine actor. Let's call him.' So we called him; Ramesh Sippy did a screen test and liked him.

NMK: Was that Amjad Khan's first film?

JA: He had played a small role in Love and God, which had not been released at that point. And he had acted in a film by Chetan Anand Sahib; I don't know which film that was. Gabbar was his first major role.

NMK: I believe Amjad Khan acted in a few films as a child actor and the film by Chetan Anand that you mentioned was the 1973 film Hindustan ki Kasam.

Did you always like being involved in the casting of your films?

JA: Oh yes, we were, particularly with directors with whom we worked closely, like Ramesh Sippy. We were one team. Sippy Films was like a family to us because we had started our career there. We were involved in the casting of even minor characters. Our suggestions were taken very seriously. It was the same with Yash Chopra. We worked very closely with these two directors.

NMK: Did you ever think that a serious casting mistake actually spoiled any of your films?

JA: I really wonder what *Shakti*'s fate would have been if the son's role had been played by some other actor who did not have Amitabh Bachchan's status. Perhaps that would have been better because the role was not big enough for Amitabh. By that time, Amitabh had become too big. I believe that *Shakti* was one of his good performances, but it's sad that many people did not appreciate his work in the film. Dilip Sahib was very good but so was Amitabh. Hats off to him! In spite of being a megastar, he did not let his stardom come in the way of playing the role of the son. And when he played the son, he looked submissive, passive, frightened, and intimidated—as a son should look in front of a powerful father. Some people confused this with some kind of weakness. He showed he's an actor first, then a star. But the fact remains that he was a superstar, and people expected more from him than the script or the role offered. But I wonder if an actor of lesser stature had played that role, perhaps *Shakti* could have been a more satisfying film.

NMK: Would you have liked *Shakti* to be without songs?

JA: Why not? Ask Mr Ramesh Sippy. I tried unsuccessfully to persuade him to remove the songs from *Shakti*. I told him, 'This film will run better and will be more respected.' I don't think the songs drew the audience to the theatre for a single show.

NMK: Going back to the question of casting, did you know that Satyajit Ray cast Amjad Khan in *Shatranj ke Khilari* after seeing him as Gabbar Singh in *Sholay*? Had you met Mr Ray?

JA: I did meet him. As a matter of fact, he said wonderful things about *Sholay*. He liked the film very much, and I'm willing to believe he cast Amjad Khan after seeing him in *Sholay*—where else could he have seen Amjad? It's stating the obvious, but Mr Ray belonged to some other league. Talking about films made in this country and talking about Ray's movies in the same breath isn't fair. [*smiles*]

I believe—and this is largely true all over the world—that cinema is still dependent on literature because it's still a very young art form. But it will soon develop and cease to depend on it as heavily. Though Satyajit Ray had adapted novels to the screen, it is only in his films that you see how cinema can transcend literature, whether it is *Pather Panchali*, *Aparajito*, or *Apur Sansar*. Personally my favourite is *Charulata*. That is cinema. Another picture that I have liked is Mrinal Sen's *Khandar*. Again, that is cinema.

NMK: Do you mean those particular stories could not be told as well in any other medium?

JA: You couldn't have told the story of *Charulata* the way Satyajit Ray narrated it on the screen.

NMK: Is story-telling an important tradition in India?

JA: You know, we once had an institution of storytellers; it has unfortunately died with time. In my childhood, I remember seeing some storytellers, but then they disappeared.

I'll tell you a true story. There was once a storyteller in Lucknow who had been narrating for many long nights a story to a nawab who suffered from insomnia. One night, the storyteller told the nawab that he wanted to go for Haj. The nawab said, 'I'll make all the arrangements for your travel, but there is one little problem, who will tell me the story?' The storyteller replied, 'I have a shaagird [disciple] who is a very competent storyteller—he has learned a lot from me—he'll continue narrating the story while I'm away.' So the nawab agreed. The storyteller called his shaagird and instructed him, 'From tomorrow, you will continue the story from this point: the king is going to battle and his armies are assembling outside the palace. The king must now ride out of the palace and lead the armies to war.' The shaagird said, 'Fine, sir, I'll continue the story from there.' The storyteller went away and returned after two months. When he came back he was very tense, so instead of going home, he went to the nawab and asked, 'Sir, I hope my shaagird has been coming here on time and doing his job properly?' The nawab replied, 'I am very happy with him. He's definitely a very good storyteller. Every night he narrated the story to me—it was wonderful. No complaints at all.' The storyteller was greatly relieved and so he went home. Later that evening, he saw his shaagird and patted him on the back, 'Well done. From tomorrow I'll continue the story. So tell me, to what point have you developed it?' The shaagird said, 'As you were travelling around the world, who was I to make the king leave the palace? Sir, from tomorrow you can continue the story from the point that you left it.' [both laugh]

NMK: In cinema, Satyajit Ray was a master storyteller. Would you have liked to work with him in his Urdu film *Shatranj ke Khilari*?

JA: There was never any opportunity to work with him. For a very long time, Shyam Benegal and I have been flirting with the idea that some day we would work together. We had even agreed to do a film, but I don't know what happened. Though I have written songs for his *Sardari Begum*.

NMK: What about directors like Ghatak?

JA: I haven't seen much of Ghatak's work so I won't venture an opinion. I think M.S. Sathyu has made an exceptionally good film in *Garam Hawa*. I liked Benegal's *Manthan*, *Ankur*, and *Nishant*—these were very good films.

NMK: You described Hindi cinema as a state within India. How would you categorize the New Cinema directors? Do they form a district or a sub-state?

JA: No, they don't belong to the state of Hindi cinema at all. They're different, they're from India! *[both laugh]*

NMK: Why do you think New Cinema does not have a big audience in India? Is it because the films have no songs, or that they are too realistic?

JA: This kind of cinema has a much smaller audience the world over. Many people believed there was an audience out there, but the lack of theatres in India, and the disinterest of theatre owners who did not release these pictures, hampered the success of New Cinema films. Then video came onto the scene. One soon realized that the middle class had no interest either in watching these films. If you go to any neighbourhood video shop and ask for a New Cinema film, it won't be available. But if you ask for *Himmatwala* or *Justice Chaudhury* or any Manmohan Desai film, they'll have it. There's no demand for New Cinema films; that's why you can't easily find them. Ten or fifteen years ago, people who owned VCRs and television sets were definitely the upper middle class and the so-called gentry of the country; and they did not encourage this cinema. I'm not saying there is no audience at all, but in the early life of New Cinema, the audience was limited. If the government wanted to do something then for parallel cinema, they should've created a market instead of creating financial corporations. The films would have eventually found their own finance. In every state, they should've built 100 small 300-seater theatres back in the 1970s and 80s.

NMK: Were you ever tempted to write a Muslim social or a script for a historical film like *Mughal-e-Azam*?

JA: *Mughal-e-Azam* is a fantasy; it has nothing to do with history. Jahangir [Prince Salim] had probably married many times and was married for the first time at eighteen.

NMK: So Anarkali never existed?

JA: There is some grave in Lahore that's supposed to be Anarkali's. There may have been some courtesan or singer who existed during Akbar's time by the name of Anarkali. That's about all. The idea of Jahangir falling in love with her and creating a rift between father and son is a story that was created in the 1920s by an Urdu playwright called Imtiaz Ali Taj. On the question of language: in Akbar's time, Urdu was not developed at all, and the lingua franca was Persian. For the people of that time, Persian was what English is to us. So all the rulers, including the Marathas, used Persian as their court language. Today, if somebody does not know English, he will be considered uneducated. Akbar did not know Persian, and that is why many historians considered him to be uneducated. Akbar was born in Sind and brought up in northern India. So most probably he spoke Haryanvi and Bhojpuri. Now if you make a movie like *Mughal-e-Azam* with Akbar the Great speaking Haryanvi or Bhojpuri, it will destroy so many myths. [*NMK laughs*]

NMK: You speak of films like *Jaal*, *Mughal-e-Azam*, or *Gunga Jumna* having affected you deeply. Do you believe any of your own films have affected others in a similar way?

JA: I think so. Even though many years have passed since *Sholay* or *Deewaar* were released, they're still relevant. On television, you see many references to these films. It means they're still in the minds of young filmmakers and in the minds of the audience. *Zanjeer*, *Deewaar*, and *Trishul* have changed the basic chemistry of the Indian hero to a great extent. There is no doubt about it. In a way, Hindi films can be regarded as contemporary folklore. And a folk hero, in any period, in any decade, is a personification of the moral values of that decade; he reflects the collective fantasies of the time. When we look at the 1930s and 1940s, we find the character of Devdas or imitations of him—these were the models of the Hindi film hero. In earlier times, the common man's morality was shaped largely through folklore, religious books, and stories. In those stories, we find that sacrifice was regarded as a great deed. And so the 1930s' and 40s' screen hero was a man who suffered, and there was heroism in enduring that suffering. If you look at the 1950s and the 1960s, you will see a gradual transformation. The hero has new ambitions and his fantasies have changed. But a change in morality takes more time. If you see Shammi Kapoor's films, or the early films of Dharmendra or Rajendra Kumar, you will see these heroes are not willing to die for the world, or for a cause, or for themselves. But the morality that they had inherited from the 1940s was not entirely worked out of their system. These heroes were the new Devdases. They were not ready to live without Paro, but they would not die for her, they would find a way of winning her. Success had become a virtue by then. But success at any price still was not admissible: that came during our time in the 1970s. It started with films like *Zanjeer* and *Deewaar*. We shed the old morality, and the new hero surfaced with another kind of morality.

NMK: But many of your heroes die at the end of the film, even though they were willing to fight the system.

JA: Someone once said, 'A hero is a person who can make a failure look magnificent.' What a wonderful thing to say.

When the hero in *Deewaar* failed, it was a magnificent failure. One admired and envied him—'I wish I could fail like this.' Devdas is a failure, but what a glamorous failure he was. He drinks himself to death and goes back to the village of his beloved and dies at her gate. What a romantic death. One would like to die like that. You can hear the audience say to one another in a hushed tone, 'Ye hai hero' [*This* is a hero].

NMK: In what way did *Deewaar* and *Zanjeer* reflect the 1970s?

JA: I can't say that when we were writing *Zanjeer* and *Deewaar*, we were aware of these connections. It would be dishonest to say that. We were part of what was happening at that time. But when I think back to *Zanjeer*'s release in 1973—that was a time when there was a sense of mistrust in society. If you considered the political mood of the country, you would have found a lot of frustration. Social protest had begun. That was the time when Jayaprakash Narayan's socialist movement had begun. Hindi films are most widely seen in the Hindi belt, and in that area, law and order was gradually breaking down. So the common man was experiencing upheaval. There was disillusionment with all the institutions, colleges, the police force. People were disillusioned with the government. So it was not surprising that the morality of the day was telling you that if you want justice, you had to fight for it yourself. No one will fight on your behalf. And if you didn't fight, you would be crushed and finished off. So Vijay, the hero of *Zanjeer*, reflected the thinking of the time. Two years later, the same Vijay is seen again in *Deewaar*. By then he has left the police force, crossed that final line, and become a smuggler. He wages war against the injustice he had to endure and emerges a winner.

You can see that the screen hero between 1973 and 1975— the Emergency was declared in India in 1975—reflected those times. I remember in Delhi or in Bombay or in Calcutta, many respectable people would boast of their great friendship with various smugglers. So, in a society in which such things are acceptable, it was no wonder that such a hero was acceptable too.

NMK: The yardstick of what is socially acceptable changes with each decade. Everyone is so careful today about not offending the sensibility of any community or group. In that light, I was curious about the temple scene in *Deewaar*, in which the hero,

Vijay, addresses Lord Shiva in an angry tone and blames him for his personal suffering. I wonder whether you could use that kind of defiance for a screen character today.

JA: As a matter of fact, when this scene was shot, we had a discussion with Amitabh Bachchan. We felt he had too harsh a tone in the scene—a bit too defiant. But he was quite convinced and said, 'If I start the dialogue on a low note, then somewhere in between I'll have to raise my tone. So instead, I'm going to start the delivery of dialogue from a very strong stance and work my way down.' I think it worked. He was right.

NMK: Could it have offended anyone?

JA: It did cross our minds at the time, but it didn't offend anyone. The credit goes to Amitabh Bachchan for approaching the scene in the way that he did. We had our doubts then, and there was definitely more than one opinion on the interpretation of the scene.

I must say you notice things very minutely, because again you're the first person who has pointed this out. And you're reminding me of things that happened many years ago. Another thing that amuses me is that in the film, Vijay buys a skyscraper for 15 lakhs and says, 'I would have paid 10 lakhs more if asked to.' With 15 lakhs, today you can't even buy a garage in Bombay to park your car!

NMK: Which of your films do you think was the most moral?

JA: [thinks carefully] Deewaar. I don't use the word 'moral' in a narrow sense but on a subconscious level. Another film that questioned morality, without giving black-and-white answers—because perhaps there were none to give—was Shakti. Shakti is perhaps a better example. It is centred on three people with different morals, and yet no one is wrong.

NMK: So it shows a more complex situation. I recently saw *Trishul* again: it seemed you needed to make the motivations of the main character extremely transparent. We see Amitabh's character state his motivations repeatedly.

JA: *Trishul* was doing things that had never been seen before. When we discuss it now, it seems so ordinary and so trivial, but something that has not been tried before is regarded as dangerous and risky for an Indian filmmaker. The hero of *Trishul* was the first 'real' illegitimate child on the Hindi screen. His parents, who are played by Sanjeev Kumar and Waheeda Rehman, are not seen going to some abandoned temple and exchanging *malas* to show they are married in the eyes of god, if not in the eyes of the world. Nor do they make love because it was raining. [*NMK laughs*] They share a mature physical relationship and that is clearly established in the film. That's how the hero's mother gets pregnant. This type of situation had never been seen before in Hindi films. Years later, the hero's mission is to destroy his own father—that too had never been seen before. When *Trishul* was released, S. Mukherjee said, 'I have seen this picture three times to try and understand why it's successful, but I can tell you that if you had come to me with this script, I would not have taken it.'

NMK: Was it for fear of the audience's reaction?

JA: Yes. Here is a hero who knowingly sets out to destroy his own father. Since we had run such a risk, we had to sanctify the hero's mission in some way. So we repeatedly reminded the audience that the son's motivation was his mother's suffering. Because his actions were breaking old taboos, we had to say, 'You see, he's doing it for his mother!' We had to keep drumming it in.

NMK: I am sure people have asked you whether there's a secret to writing a successful film or script.

JA: They do, and I say that I don't know the answer. But I can tell you two ways of writing an *unsuccessful* film. First, you decide you'll make a great film, and second, you decide the film you're making is not for you but for the common man, a film for the masses. In the first situation, you're looking upwards and in the other, you're looking down. You go wrong because in both cases you're going to create something that is not coming from you. The films that work well are those that have been made with total conviction and enthusiasm. I am sure that people who have worked on those films, whether writers, directors, or actors, thoroughly enjoyed the whole experience. You cannot make a successful film cold-bloodedly—that's impossible. When Manmohan Desai made *Amar Akbar Anthony*, I am quite sure that he enjoyed every minute; and so did K. Asif when he was making *Mughal-e-Azam*. If you are enjoying your work, it will reach people. But if you think, 'This is the kind of film that works at the box office'—that cold-blooded quality seeps through the film. It shows when you're trying to manipulate—and it doesn't work. I've noticed that whenever I've tried to manipulate, I've failed. I fail when I try to be clever instead of digging into my psyche or into my fantasies. When I wrote scripts that depended on my reputation and depended on craft and memory—they didn't work.

NMK: If you were very honest, which of your scripts comes to mind when you say that?

JA: *Roop ki Rani Choron ka Raja* is the prime example. *Shaan*.

NMK: Do you think you were aware of it at the time?

JA: You can't be totally aware of it or you wouldn't do it. But somewhere, you feel something is wrong. Because you're deprived of that joy, that pleasure you had when you worked with total sincerity. Though you try to take confident stances, somewhere in your heart, you know it is not genuine.

For example, when I'm working, as I sometimes do, in a hotel room and am writing a tragic scene, I get tears in my eyes. When I'm writing a lighter scene, I smile or laugh. When this scene goes to the director, he gives it to an actor, then the actor will perform it, the camera will film it, an editor will edit it, then it will be sent to different cities like Ratlam, Sanghli, or Jabalpur. And in Jabalpur, a man who has never met me, and who will never meet me, will buy a ticket and see the film. If I had cried in that hotel room while writing a scene, it will touch him. And if I hadn't, it won't. Although I am not directly communicating the scene to him, yet my sincerity or insincerity gets conveyed in spite of all the different interpreters. You just can't fool people. I don't know how it happens, but it happens—when writing poetry, short stories, novels, or even when writing a letter.

NMK: There seems to be a very fine balance between personal experience—what you feel in that hotel room—and a universal emotion. Have you ever taken a story directly from a real-life event or from a newspaper article and used it in a script?

JA: I have used real events in sequences and scenes, but not a whole plot. I have many examples, but the one that comes to mind was a very strange and interesting theft at Tribhovandas—the biggest jewellery shop in Bombay. I read about that incident in the paper and worked it into a sequence in *Khel*.

NMK: I'm wondering if you've seen any of your films again in recent years? What still works for you? And what doesn't?

JA: [*long pause*] For a long time, I hadn't seen any. A few years ago, I saw *Deewaar*, and I also saw a part of *Main Azaad Hoon* when it was playing on a cable channel.

NMK: Didn't you receive *Filmfare*'s Best Dialogue Writer Award for *Main Azaad Hoon*?

JA: Yes. The film had a large number of characters, and I tried to make each character speak in a different style.

NMK: Do you think *Deewaar* still works?

JA: *Deewaar* has a very good screenplay. Heavy, but good.

NMK: It seems you were not allowed too much reality in the 1970s. Though *Deewaar* may have reflected the tensions of its time, realism in commercial cinema is not really encouraged. Though you see it creeping into the storylines of the 1990 films.

JA: Creeping is the right word. It's entering the films very slowly. The airtight world of Hindi cinema is breaking down slightly.

NMK: *Deewaar*'s dialogue is still superb and so was Amitabh.

JA: Yes, he was.

NMK: A lot of people thought when you and Salim Khan were writing that you had Amitabh in mind—is this true? And if so, are there advantages working with an actor who has a particular style?

JA: First of all, it's not true. Films like *Zanjeer* or *Deewaar* were not written with Amitabh in mind. It's true in the case of *Trishul* and *Kaala Patthar*. We knew Amitabh would be cast. When we were writing *Shakti*, we didn't know that Amitabh Bachchan would be in the film—we had no idea. Many other factors and coincidences meant that Amitabh was cast in the film. *Shakti* was basically a vehicle for Dilip Kumar; it was planned for him, not for Amitabh. Even if we knew Amitabh would be cast in *Trishul*, or *Kaala Patthar,* or *Don*, we did not write the scripts of those films nor did we ever write any script that would end up being a showcase of his talents and his acting prowess. This fact helped us, but it harmed us too. At a certain stage, he had become such a big star that if we had written roles tailor-made for him, perhaps it would have helped us and those pictures would have done well just on the strength of his stardom. But we never did that. We never wrote pictures for any star.

NMK: But knowing who will be cast must be an advantage when writing?

JA: If you know that such and such actor is going to play a role, you should always keep his or her plus and minus points in mind. There are certain actors who do not look particularly appealing if they cry or are emotional, and there are other actors who do those kinds of scenes well. So within the given narrative, it's good if you can create a situation, treat a scene in which you imbibe and involve the actor's strengths, or avoid or hide an actor's weaker points. The the ideal situation is that an actor and a script should meet each other halfway. You shouldn't write a script for a star. Start writing a character and then think of the best person to play the character. The script should offer certain scenes and situations to the actor; scenes that he or she has not done before. That's how the actor gets energy or strength from a screenplay. If you rely completely on star image, you'll end up making the actor do what he's done many times before. It will harm the actor because the law of diminishing utility will affect the star, and your film will look second-hand and trite.

NMK: What do you feel Amitabh's great asset is?

JA: I am an unconditional Amitabh Bachchan fan. I genuinely believe that he's a very fine actor. I think that ultimately commercial cinema was not big enough to give him any real challenge. The framework of commercial cinema was too restrictive, and Amitabh too tall. So each time he had to make himself smaller. Perhaps after 1977, after *Amar Akbar Anthony*, I'd say that he did not do any film that challenged him as an actor. *Zanjeer* was a challenge and so was *Deewaar*; *Amar Akbar Anthony* is also a very important film in Amitabh Bachchan's career. But after that, I don't think he discovered anything new in himself as an actor.

People kept seeing what they had seen before, and they enjoyed it thoroughly. That's why he has remained a superstar for so many years. But what role scared him into thinking, 'Will I be able to do this?' He was scared while doing *Zanjeer*, or *Deewaar*, or even for that matter, *Amar Akbar Anthony*. These were real challenges for him. And he faced the challenges so well, but not after 1977.

NMK: Why did that happen?

JA: They trapped him in his star image—and I would say that he accepted this trap willingly.

NMK: One does get trapped. Did you find that the same thing was happening to you and to Salim Khan?

JA: The same thing *was* happening to us. The 1970s was the high point in our careers, and after that the quality of our work deteriorated. I wish we had kept the same energy. After 1975–6, our scripts lost that intensity. I don't think our work was very good after the mid-1970s. I could see it.

NMK: The fire was not raging any more. I suppose it can't burn that intensely forever.

JA: I suppose not. There could be many reasons. You can become complacent. You lose that hunger, you start feeling secure within the formula. You think this is what is expected of you, and you think this is what works because it has always worked. It will work again and that spirit of adventure, that daring quality, that devil-may-care attitude eventually disappears.

NMK: So you think that success can be damaging to creativity?

JA: Yes, of course. I think it happened in our case. If we had the right scripts, Amitabh would have done anything that we offered him, without question. But what did we offer him? After *Trishul* and *Don*, we failed as writers. We didn't do anything worthwhile.

NMK: You're being very harsh on yourself.

JA: It's a fact. *Dostana* was a very big hit—at best it was a competent film. *Zamana* was a very bad film. Even today, I feel that *Kaala Patthar* could have been much better. *Shaan*, *Dostana*—that's what we gave Amitabh. Somewhere, we had lost that intensity and that quality. We could have offered him good roles—but we were not the only writers in the world—he should've looked around. [*laughs*]

NMK: Do you think that Amitabh Bachchan would have had a greater choice of roles in Hollywood? Was he restricted by the formula of Hindi cinema?

JA: I suppose you can't become a very big star without having a very strong image, and you can't have a strong image if you insist on variety and versatility. It's very strange that whilst De Niro is widely respected, it's Sylvester Stallone and Clint Eastwood who are the bigger stars. As far as star image is concerned, you have to kind of specialize in a particular mould. But I think Amitabh could have created a little more elbowroom for himself than he did.

NMK: His colleagues did not help either. The writers, the directors, the producers didn't help; they seemed to want him to repeat himself.

JA: I think what goes wrong is that we get too scared of failing. When you're too scared of failing, you don't experiment. And when you don't experiment, you tend to become trite.

NMK: When you wrote *Zanjeer* and *Deewaar,* you were experimenting, you were young. You were close in age to the vast majority of the audience.

JA: You see, we weren't bothered. We weren't bothered whether our scripts were conforming to the norm. But ultimately we started to bother.

NMK: As you said, Hindi cinema is like another state in India. And I suppose what happens is that, as with everyone, you want to start belonging too. You did not want to be in the margins but integrated in the mainstream.

JA: [*laughs*] Yes, I suppose so.

NMK: If you had the chance now, is there any film ending you would rewrite?

JA: [*thinks for a while*] I went wrong towards the end of *Mashaal*...there are many pictures that I would like to rewrite.

NMK: In hindsight, what did you learn from a film that was less successful?

JA: [*long pause*] From *Kaala Patthar* I learned that instead of sitting in a hotel room and writing about a coal mine, if we had treated the script a little more realistically, it would have worked better. Either you don't use a realistic plot or a realistic locale in the first place, or if you do, you have to be very convincing.

NMK: Because you set up an expectation.

Were you depressed when some films didn't work?

JA: There's no point in being depressed about things. One should learn. If you're learning, you won't get depressed. When a sense of loss overtakes you and you forget about learning anything because you think everything is lost, then you get depressed. But I feel one is always prone to new mistakes, different mistakes. What's important is that you should work from your heart with total sincerity and involvement. Do what excites you; don't do things that you *think* are the right thing to do.

NMK: When did you decide to stop writing screenplays?

JA: [*pause*] I can't tell you the exact moment or the date or the day. But I was becoming mechanical. Producers were paying me so I had to write. There was no excitement or sense of achievement or discovery. It wasn't there. So I thought I'd give myself a break. And when I get excited again, then I'll write scripts again.

NMK: On the question of violence in films, do you think you and Salim Khan introduced something that was undesirable?

JA: Action in cinema has always been very appealing all over the world. It thrills audiences. When I tell people there was more footage showing fight scenes in *Bobby* than in *Deewaar*, they are surprised. *Deewaar* only had one fight, in the garage. That's all. There was no other fight in the film.

NMK: Do you think you managed to retain in your work a sense of the tehzeeb [culture] that you grew up with?

JA: There's a saying in Urdu, if you want to know somebody well, either live with them for 14 years or travel with them. But there's another way: observe a person when he or she is very angry. People drop their guard in a moment of anger—their real self is revealed. No matter how angry you are, if you are a decent person, you won't say or do things that you believe unfair or below the belt. That's where your class will show.

In our films, we dealt with anger, especially in the characters played by Amitabh Bachchan. But you will see a certain grace about that character. That's important, and that reflects one's upbringing. This applies to Amitabh's background too. So many other actors have tried to ape Amitabh, but they've failed. Because they didn't have the sophistication and the tehzeeb that Amitabh grew up with. As an actor, Amitabh's anger was never ugly. Other actors mix anger with arrogance. But Amitabh's anger was mixed with hurt and tears. So you accepted it, you were fascinated by it, and you found justification for it. But I'm afraid in later pictures even Amitabh developed that arrogance.

NMK: Are you interested in people? Do you have a lot of close friends?

JA: No, I don't have very close friends, but I am interested in people. There's nothing more interesting than people. But I have a weakness for people who are bright and have a good sense of humour. I have respect for nice people, but I'd rather spend an evening with an *interesting* person. *[both laugh]*

NMK: Talking about interesting people, if you had the chance, would you have liked to write a script for Raj Kapoor or Mehboob Khan?

JA: Perhaps more so for Mehboob, because I share Mehboob's sense of drama more than I share Raj Kapoor's idea of drama.

NMK: How would you define the difference?

JA: There is something more masculine about Mehboob Khan's concept of drama. It's stronger. When you see *Mother India*, or *Andaaz*, or *Amar*, you'll find the structures of his scripts were based on solid, metallic girders. While Raj Kapoor would use silken threads—that's the difference. There was something delicate about Raj Kapoor's scripts, very sensitive; but the central point of Raj Kapoor's sensibility was not very masculine. In my style of prose writing, I find I am closer to Mehboob's kind of work. In no way am I undermining Raj Kapoor, but it is a matter of language, expression, and one's own sensibility. When you see my films, you'll say, 'Yes, that's right.' They are closer to Mehboob's pictures in attitude, in wavelength, and in the style of communication. The difference between these two directors is similar to the difference between oil painting and watercolours. Who says watercolours are inferior? They're not. But oil painting has a kind of depth. Even in a script, or in writing, you can have that same quality.

NMK: You mean bold strokes. Definite characters. Both Mehboob Khan's *Andaaz* and Raj Kapoor's *Awaara* were very important films in the evolution of Indian cinema—they introduced modernity in Indian film. Did these films have any impact on you?

JA: As a matter of fact, these pictures were not a part of my development. When *Andaaz* and *Awaara* were released, I was too young. I don't remember their release at all.

NMK: It's interesting to note that despite the so-called love of formula, the films that are remembered—like *Andaaz* or *Awaara*—are precisely the ones that broke the norm and introduced a new spin, or a character that reflects his or her time. How do you introduce new elements in the usual formula film? Take, for example, a scene that you see often in Hindi films, in which the hero is going for a job interview. How could you show that situation in your films?

JA: It depended on many things. The first situation that comes to mind is that perhaps the hero of the film is trying to enter the corporate world. I don't think this thought would have come to me in the 1970s. Like in *Deewaar*, when Shashi Kapoor tries to find a job, he goes to a jeweller's shop. You remember? Today if I wrote a similar scene, I would take him to a much grander set-up.

NMK: The social context has gone up a few notches. Now screen characters have to be part of the big time.

JA: Yes! Perhaps the corporate world would not give him a job because they don't find him sufficiently sophisticated or Westernized. In the 1990s, the average small-town man could feel marginalized in the big city because this vast corporate world is developing around him and is unknown to him. He's an outsider in every sense of the word. He doesn't know the ways of this new world. So perhaps that is the environment I'd show when representing the 1990s.

Most Indians would have identified with him. Somewhere within our reach there is opportunity, but we can't avail ourselves of it because we're different from 'them'. So the dramatic bite comes from this opposition: the 'we' and the 'them'.

NMK: I wonder if you could write a *Deewaar* today and set it in contemporary times. The divide today is not only between the haves and the have-nots but also between the old way of working and the new computerized world.

JA: More importantly, I don't know if I could find that kind of intensity and anger—that thrust that made us write *Deewaar*.

NMK: Is it a thrust for change? A desire to change the world? Is that what audiences today aspire to?

JA: At this moment, people are looking for something else. If a film like *Deewaar* was released now, I don't think it would set a trend the way it did in its time. *Deewaar*'s dilemmas are no longer big problems. At the moment, people are experiencing socio-political chaos. There is no well-defined establishment before them. Strange things are happening, they are bewildered. Today's people are looking for a balm. The feel-good factor. They're tired of anger, and even tired of being cynical. They want to see things that are nice and gentle. Pleasant things that will settle upon their nerves like a feather. That's a feeling I share too.

NMK: In films like *Virasat* and *Border*, there is a greater degree of technical polish in lighting, photography, and so on. And in some ways, Hindi cinema is more reflective of reality. For example, the dialogue is closer to the way people talk. Another new element is that love is seen as something possible in marriage. In *Virasat*, a love relationship develops

after marriage, and there's also a sense in the movies that
men and women are working towards being equals. And if
two women are seen to love the same man, they do not have
to be rivals.

JA: Things are changing.

NMK: The other side of the coin is a film like *Dil to Pagal
Hai*, which seems to present a composite world that excludes
India. When Madhuri Dixit steps out of her house, she's in
Scotland. When Akshay Kumar goes for a day trip supposedly
from India, he lands up in Holland.

JA: This film offers a totally alternate reality. It has nothing to
do with reality. I appreciate it because it's not pretending to be
real. It offers a comic book kind of pretty love story. It's a world
of its own. There's no harm in that.

NMK: Producers always say, but I don't know how true it is,
that audiences want fantasy in cinema.

JA: If the audience wanted these kinds of films, then why do
most of them fail? The percentage of successful films is very,
very low. As a matter of fact, the films that conform a hundred
per cent to what the audiences are supposed to want, more
often than not, fail. Pictures that offer something that audience
do not want do better. For example, *Roop ki Rani Choron ka Raja*
had everything that audiences were supposed to want—that is
according to the distributors and producers—so what did the
film lack? It didn't have sincerity, it didn't have what you call
'soul', because it was not heartfelt. Things don't work if they
aren't heartfelt. That's for sure.

NMK: I suppose audiences want to be surprised—in spite of
the fact that they also expect formula.

JA: You have to offer some new element in every film.
Something must be new—even if the rest of the film is formulaic.

NMK: You mean a new spin? What about the so-called market forces that compel producers to think they must make the same film again and again?

JA: They don't know anything. A good product finds its own market, it creates a market. You have to decide whether you want to make a thing for the market or you want to make a market for the thing. [*NMK laughs*] There is no guarantee that if you make a film this way or that, it will be a success. And since there are no guarantees, make the film the way you'd like to make it. So at least there will be one person who likes the film—that's you! [*laughs*] If you make your film with some sensibility and feeling and some intelligence, you'll make something that will be liked by some people. But if you try to please everybody, you generally wind up pleasing no one.

NMK: The 1990s' films seem to put all their energies into dance, music, and light-heartedness. The heroes of these films appear to be the grandchildren of Shammi Kapoor, and seem modelled on the hero in the 1961 film *Junglee*. Why did light romance become such a favourite theme again?

JA: John Ford once said, 'If you're confused, make a Western.' In the same way, in India whenever we are confused, we hide behind romance, because romance is universal. As I've said, the hero is the personification of contemporary morality and aspirations. If you're unclear what the contemporary morality is, how can you have a strong character? Male or female. After Amitabh's 'angry young man', Indian cinema has not been able to develop another code or set of morals that could create another strong hero-image. Perhaps that is why the 1990s' hero is preoccupied with comedy and romance.

NMK: If you say heroes reflect contemporary morality, then it seems that audiences *do* want some reality in Hindi films.

This may have contributed to the huge success your 1970s films enjoyed. After an era dominated by light, romantic films came *Zanjeer*—unlike New Cinema films it retained the conventions of Hindi cinema entertainment, and had action, songs, romance, drama. I have a hunch that films like *Border* and *Virasat* will be remembered because they touch reality like *Zanjeer* did in its time.

JA: Personally I feel that after the 'angry young man' image, the only thing that has happened that has a certain significance— and are sort of milestones—are Sooraj Barjatya's films, *Maine Pyar Kiya* and *Hum Aapke Hain Kaun*; Aditya Chopra's *Dilwale Dulhania Le Jaayenge* and Karan Johar's *Kuch Kuch Hota Hai*. These are extremely important films and should be studied with a keen eye. They are the only films after *Zanjeer* and *Deewaar* that have created a new formula, a new sensibility, a new recipe.

NMK: What is this recipe?

JA: I am quite sure that these young directors are quite unconscious about what they've done. When we wrote our scripts, we weren't conscious of the process that lay behind them. Sooraj Barjatya must have written the scripts for his films because he liked them and enjoyed them. His work is in sync with contemporary India and that's why these pictures have become very big hits. This onslaught of consumerism, the existence of multiple television and satellite channels, modernization, and industrialization have brought Indian society to a point where we are feeling slightly lost. We talk of cultural invasion, of an excess of Westernization, of the loss of family values, the loss of warmth, compassion, and love. But, on the other hand, what's the alternative? Do I go back to the village? Shall I ask the cable-man to disconnect these multiple channels? Should I stop watching Star TV, should I wear a dhoti–kurta, and never touch a Coke or Pepsi and drink only lassi?

NMK: And throw away the mobile phone!

JA: What a dilemma! What confusion! Shall I deny myself all these things? Western culture and glitter are very attractive. So *Maine Pyar Kiya* and *Hum Aapke Hain Kaun* offer the solution: a happy marriage between the two worlds. I can have everything offered by modernization and hold on to family values and tradition at the same time.

NMK: The best of both worlds.

JA: It makes me feel good. Life can be wonderful without losing either world. It's a very clever mix and appeals today to everyone facing a dilemma. The paradox is solved in these films.

NMK: Film stories are usually repetitive. But how does a writer know when he's allowed to repeat a style of dialogue precisely because that particular brand of wit is what the audience comes back for? And when he'll be rejected precisely because he is repeating himself?

JA: There's no foolproof way of knowing. But again, as long as you're enjoying it, it remains enjoyable. When the work follows a formula—formula 44, formula 43—then it doesn't work. As long as *you* are thrilled about it, somehow this thrill is contagious and impacts others.

NMK: Do you think awareness and self-consciousness of style actually starts killing it?

JA: To be interesting, you have to be interested. If you are involved yourself, you're bound to involve others. As you become more professional, two things may happen: one is that you become mechanical and that you develop a facility to quickly connect to the right reservoirs of emotion and apply it to the scene at hand. That's fine. But what might also happen is that you are left only with your craft and no emotions. I think there is no watertight compartment between the person and the artist, so if it's alive in the person, it will be alive in the artist.

NMK: But the people who surround artists or stars flatter them too much. And though it must be reassuring in many ways for the star, it's also dangerous.

JA: Very dangerous. I think if you continue to look at your work with objectivity, it will keep humility alive in you. As long as you have a sense of incompleteness, you'll have a certain edge in your effort.

NMK: Hindi cinema has a mass appeal in Africa and in many other continents. Why do you think that is?

JA: Hindi films have a mass appeal in Latin America too, particularly in smaller towns and rural areas. In the big cities, Hollywood wins. So I suppose there is something about this cinema that appeals to the Third World.

NMK: Is it the importance of religion, the importance of family? Why does it not appeal to a 'white' audience?

JA: For our audience, the importance of family and very clearly defined emotions matter. When *Mother India* was released in London in the 1950s, I believe some English critic reviewed it and the title of the review was: 'Flood, Blood, Mud with Mother!' [*both laugh*]

NMK: I read a review somewhere in which an American critic had said that the mother character, Radha, played by Nargis, was very cruel because she lets her children starve instead of marrying the moneylender.

JA: And living happily ever after. Yes!

NMK: Why didn't you write strong roles for women, like the Radha character in *Mother India*?

JA: So many times people have asked why Salim Sahib and I did not write woman-oriented scripts. It's true, we didn't. At the same time, you have to give us credit that our female characters, whether in *Deewaar*, *Trishul*, *Shakti*, or *Sholay*, are very independent-minded women. More often than not, they are working women. They are anything but docile, submissive, and passive. So instead of making a film like *Main Chup Rahungi*, in which you show a woman as a doormat, I think it's better to write a male-oriented film in which a woman has dignity, even if she has a small role to play in the narrative. We did break new ground in *Trishul*: it's the first film in which the heroine sleeps with the man in her life without feeling guilty. The relationship between the characters played by Waheeda Rehman and Sanjeev Kumar is a mature one. That's true even of the character played by Parveen Babi in *Deewaar*. If I were to write a script today, my women characters would be even more mature, more independent, more liberated because my perspective on the question has become slightly clearer. When I see *Seeta aur Geeta*, there's a scene in it that makes me cringe. Geeta, who's actually Seeta, has started cooking extremely well and can also sew. So everyone thinks she's become a model girl as a result. Today, I'd write her character very differently. The way I wrote the Seeta character then wasn't intentional, but it came from my understanding at that point in time.

NMK: What is your understanding now?

JA: I believe it is a matter of time before women take over the world. For thousands of years, women have been confined to a very small area of life. When you have a small canvas to work with, you develop an eye for detail. The world is changing and technology has made all the physical advantages of man over woman obsolete. Today what is required in the age of computers is precisely an eye for detail. So I believe the woman is the future and the man is becoming obsolete.

NMK: I like the fact that you were not pretending to be a pro-feminist in the 1970s. Was your wife, Shabana Azmi, instrumental in your becoming sensitized to women's issues?

JA: The people around you always contribute to your development. The women who have entered my life have always been extremely strong, independent—people in their own right. But a conservative attitude towards women was common currency in Hindi films, so without realizing the implications or connotations, I wrote that scene. Now I would not.

NMK: The image of the Indian woman has changed over the years. How would you define that change? Let's compare a character Meena Kumari played in the 1950s with a Madhuri Dixit screen character of the 1990s.

JA: The educated Indian male knows beyond any doubt that the woman portrayed by Meena Kumari is obsolete. But this middle-class conservative man, or woman for that matter, has yet to understand who the new woman is. No one is clear on this. What kind of freedom is right and what is wrong? So you see pictures that show a peculiar bravado like the film *Ek Pal*. I personally found it a pretty stupid film. After seeing the film, I told Kalpana Lajmi, the director, 'Here's a woman married to a big official who works in a tea estate. This woman lives in a huge house and when her husband goes to work, she feels lonely and walks from room to room with a glass of cognac in her hand, sits near a piano, or languishes near a window.' Meanwhile her poor husband works all day, while this parasite revels in self-pity. When her husband goes to Tokyo, she calls her ex-lover over, sleeps with him, and lo and behold, she's pregnant. Her lover, who had made it clear that there were no strings attached to their reunion, now says, 'I'll make the arrangements for an abortion.' She gets very upset and gives him a long lecture about the moon and the stars, and why there are so many waves in the ocean. That poor fellow goes away totally confused, just like I was. [*laughs*] Then she tells her old parents that she's carrying a child by another man. I mean she almost gives her parents a cardiac arrest. So our heroine delivers her child. The husband returns and is extremely thrilled, but our liberated woman tells him, 'This is not your child. Now it is up to you to accept this child or not. I could not lie to you.' What kind of stupid woman is she? I have no sympathy for her. Not because she has slept out of wedlock, I don't care a damn for that, but she should be smart enough not to tell her husband and her parents. What was the point of traumatizing her old parents? What kind of truth and honesty is this? Okay, if she must speak out—then let her tell her husband, but why make her poor parents suffer? [*JA gets increasingly irritated*] Her frustration is that she isn't doing anything with her life, and she has got everything on a platter. She can't solve her problems by sleeping around. Why doesn't she go out and work? I have no interest or sympathy with these kinds of confused characters.

Many people look at me with suspicion because they themselves are not clear what liberation is. We know that the old morality is obsolete, but we're unclear what the new one is. Sometimes a film like *Silsila* appears—which again is made by people who are not very clear about this new morality. They try to be brave and then they pull back. Two steps forward and three steps back. You see confusion. Why don't we have big female stars today? Take talented girls like Madhuri Dixit or Sridevi— their whole careers have been wasted singing songs and dancing. How many dramatic roles have they been offered? Very few. They deserve many more. But why is that not possible? Because there are no clear-cut dramatic roles. You can only create larger-than-life roles if you have a clear sense of morality.

NMK: Is that why a film like *Mother India* cannot be made today?

JA: Yes, and neither can films like *Main Chup Rahungi*. Strong female roles are rare. *Arth* showed some kind of clarity and offered the heroine a good role and so a good performance came out of it.

NMK: When Shabana approaches a role, do you think she is analytical or intuitive? Have you ever written dialogue for her?

JA: I wrote for her in *Main Azaad Hoon*. I think Shabana is growing as an actress. She's becoming more and more analytical. She doesn't show it and would rather [*laughs*] let others believe that she doesn't prepare, but I think a lot of thinking goes into her characterization, a lot of hard work. If she has to play a particular kind of a role, she makes sure to familiarize herself with the environment in which such a character would exist in real life.

NMK: When someone lives an extreme situation in life, and emotions are heightened, in that light Hindi film dialogue seems to ring true to life. It's almost as if your worst nightmare is articulated.

JA: We are a very theatrical people. We're not at peace with ourselves. I genuinely believe that to a great extent communalism too is based on personal unhappiness because people are personally unhappy and bitter. If they faced their own lot, they'd have to do something about it; instead they join with others and hate some other community. And their hatred gets released. They feel safer in larger groups, and feel that's a way of cleansing themselves of their own traumas and bitterness.

NMK: Do you think you're an emotional person?

JA: [*long pause*] Yes. At the same time, I'd like to believe that I am an extremely rational person. However, the fact remains that the major decisions I have made in my life have been emotional ones. But I survived them because most of the time, I'm very rational. [*smiles*]

TALKING SONGS

NMK: Very few people have managed to start off in one field—in your case—screenplay writing, reach the top of their game, and then choose a completely different direction—songwriting. Did this interest in songs start in school or college?

JA: I think it was in 1967 when the song 'Puppet on a String' was very popular. Some friends and I were discussing how Indian music directors copied tunes. I said 'Puppet on a String' had a very good tune and could be made into a good Hindi song.

Just for a laugh, I wrote some lines based on the tune of this song. [sings]

O yun dil ko jalaake sataake mita ke
Chale ho kahan
Ban ke ji tan ke ji tad ke
Chale ho kahan
Baahen rokengi meri raahen tumhaari aaj
Tum maano ya na maano tum pe hai mera raaj
[You burn my heart, taunt me, destroy me
Where are you going?
All dolled up
Where are you going?
Today my arms will hold you back
Whether you accept it or not, I rule your heart]

NMK: It's very sweet. Charming! When you were growing up, which period of Hindi film songs first caught your attention?

JA: Mainly the 1950s' music. In my school days and college days, there were no cassette players, you know. The only way we could hear a song was by going to the movies or listening to the radio sitting in a modest restaurant. We would hear popular shows of the time like *Binaca Geet Mala*, *Pancharangi Geet Mala*, and *Jai Mala*. The boys and girls of my age used to learn the songs by heart and sing them. That's how we became familiar with film music.

I'm a great fan of S.D. Burman, so if you asked me about his films—*Nau Do Gyarah, Sujata, Paying Guest, Chalti Ka Naam Gaadi,* and so many other pictures for that matter—I could tell you the names of all the songs on the album of those films. I can still recall hundreds of songs.

NMK: What do the old songs evoke in you?

JA: The songs of the 1950s and 1960s are not just songs for me—they are much more than that. They evoke so many memories. When I hear 'Jeevan ke safar mein raahi milte hain bichhad jaane ko' [On the journey of life, travellers meet only to part] from *Munimji,* it's like meeting a childhood friend. When I hear the song, I think of my schooldays, my old friends, my first girlfriend. A song brings a flood of memories. Something recorded today cannot do that. It is incapable of evoking that kind of nostalgia in me.

NMK: Did you do any serenading yourself, say, to your first girlfriend?

JA: If I answered this question, you would know why I constantly refer to 'Ye raat ye chaandni phir kahaan' [This moonlit night may never return], so I would rather not answer this one. [*both laugh*]

NMK: You mentioned listening to songs on the radio. What was the first record you owned?

JA: We had a gramophone. I mean, my mother had a gramophone, and I inherited it when she died. So I had a gramophone, but no records. It was only when I was in Aligarh, living in my aunt's house—I think I was twelve or thirteen—when I managed to buy my first 78-rpm record. It was a HMV record from the film *Kanhaiya* [1959]. All records were produced by HMV in those days. On one side was the Mukesh solo, 'Mujhe tum se kuchh bhi naa chaahiye, mujhe mere haal pe chhod do' [I want nothing from you, leave me in the state I am], and on the other side, there was Asha Bhonsle's song, 'O kanhaiya o kanhaiya, aaj aana khwaab mein' [Lord Krishna, come to me in a dream]. I bought the record because of 'Mujhe tum se kuchh bhi naa chaahiye', a song I had first heard on the radio.

NMK: When you got that record, did you listen to it again and again?

JA: I had no choice. That was the only record I owned. [both laugh] I don't know what the second record was, but I know I did not own three records—that's for sure. I remember those old gramophones had small steel needles, and after using the needle four or five times, you had to sharpen it on a stone to use it again.

NMK: Film music is hugely important in India. Is there something about songs that stirs the Indian psyche in a special way?

JA: I think a song is a release. When you sing, you're releasing repressed emotions, feelings, and thoughts. In prose, you are somehow held responsible, but in songs, you can express yourself without feeling accountable.

If you question why people fall in love, someone is bound to ask you what you have against love. But if you sing a song with words like 'Jaane kyun log pyaar karte hain?' [Who knows why people fall in love?], my song from Dil Chahta Hai, no one is going to ask for an explanation. You're allowed to express the desire to make such statements through a song without being checked.

I think the more repressed you are, the more expression you'll find in song. In societies where there is repression, you'll find a greater number of songs. It's unsurprising that in Indian society, which is largely repressive, songs from a woman's point of view are more common than songs from a man's point of view. The poor have more songs than the rich. The folk song is ultimately created, nurtured, and preserved by the poor. If the song were indeed a symbol of pleasure or luxury, there should have been more songs in affluent societies. But the fact is that the working and deprived classes have a greater number of songs.

I also believe the act of singing is a form of sexual sublimation. So if a society is sexually repressed, you'll have many more songs and more singing.

NMK: How would you define a perfect Hindi film song?

JA: An obvious and simple definition—I'd say a perfect song would have good words, composition, orchestration, and good rendering. But how does one define 'good words', 'composition', or 'good rendering'? It's all relative. The answer will vary and is a matter of personal aesthetics. But one can see that a song that depicts a particular mood or human situation will have the most appeal. A song should have a personal touch and mean something to an individual—it should touch a chord not just with the individual who is writing the song or the actor in the movie who performs it onscreen, but anyone who listens to it should be able to identify with it.

NMK: What songs have you considered perfect?

JA: There are many. 'Ye raat ye chaandni phir kahaan' [This moonlit night may never return] from *Jaal*, 'Jaane kya tu ne kahi, jaane kya main ne suni, baat kuchh ban hi gayi' [Who knows what you said, who knows what I heard. Something stirred in my heart] from *Pyaasa*, 'O sajana, barkha bahaar aayi' [O beloved, the spring showers are here] from *Parakh*.

The tune, the words, the composition, the orchestration, the singing—they're flawless songs. You would not want a single thing changed.

NMK: Do you ever feel envious—wishing that you had written one of those perfect songs?

JA: I have felt that many times. There are many great songs of the past. I think Sahir [Ludhianvi] and Shailendra have written songs that make you go 'wow!'

NMK: Absolutely. Do you think it's the melody or the lyrics that give a song a long lifespan?

JA: I can cite hundreds of songs that were instant hits but don't have great words. These songs usually fade away. Songs that last for decades are those with very good words—they are the songs you will never forget. Take again 'Ye raat ye chaandni phir kahaan'. In the same metre, you could have: 'Aaja aaja sajna, sun ja mere baalma' [Come, come, sweetheart, listen to me]—the words are on the same tune and metre, but do you think we would have remembered it?

NMK: Why did you decide to write songs in the 1980s?

JA: It was someone else's decision. I had started writing poetry in the late 1970s, but the poems were not published, except once in the Hindi literary magazine, Dharmyug. That was because the editor, Dr Dharamvir Bharati, was a family friend. I think he had published a poem and four ghazals of mine.

I used to recite my poetry only to a close circle of friends and did not attend mushairas [poetry symposia]. The few people who were somewhat familiar with my poetry included Yash Chopra. As luck would have it, the hero of his next film, Silsila, happened to be a poet. Yash Chopra always liked using poetry in his films. He had not chosen a lyricist—and I later heard—that he discussed the matter with Lata Mangeshkar. She said,

'I have not heard Javed's poetry, but Padma Sachdev, who is a very important poetess in Dogri, praises it a lot. So why not take him? Besides, he has already worked with you as a scriptwriter.'

So Yash Chopra came to me sometime in 1980 asking me to write the songs for *Silsila*. Until then I had not thought of writing songs, and as a matter of fact, at first I refused, saying, 'I'm a scriptwriter and want to stay one. Poetry is something I do for myself. I don't want to be a lyric writer.' Mr Yash Chopra is an extremely charming and persuasive person, and he succeeded in convincing me.

But I was not really sure if I could write lyrics on an existing tune—I had never done it before. So I went to Yash Chopra's house around 10.30 one morning and was introduced to the music composers, Pandit Shivkumar Sharma, who is the best santoor player we have, and Pandit Hariprasad Chaurasia, who is the best flute player in the country. They were writing music for a film for the first time. Yash Chopra explained the scene in which the song would take place, and how he planned to film it in the tulip fields near Amsterdam.

By the time I returned home that same evening, the song had been written on Shiv-Hari's tune. It was 'Dekha ek khwaab to ye silsile hue, door tak nigaahon mein hain gul khiley hue. Ye gilaa hai aap ki nigaahon se, phool bhi ho darmiyaan to faasiley hue' [Male voice: I saw a dream that brought us close. All I can now see are flowers in bloom. Female voice: I have this complaint against what you see. Even flowers can create an unwanted distance between us].

That was the first song I ever wrote, thanks to Yash Chopra.

NMK: Did you write the dialogue for *Silsila*?

JA: No, just the songs. I think the composers had to change the tune of 'Dekha ek khwaab' a little to make it work better with the words. In those days, I did not have much experience of writing to a tune. There was a certain curve towards the end of the tune, and the words I wrote did not have those curves. Instead, if I had written [*JA sings*] 'Dil ne tera naam gun gunaya hai' [My heart hummed your name], it would have worked. But the composers liked the original line so much that they adjusted the tune accordingly.

There were two other songs in the film that were written to the tune, 'Ye kahaan aa gaye hum?' [Where has love brought us?] and 'Neela aasman so gaya' [The blue sky has fallen asleep].

NMK: 'Neela aasmaan' sounds very close to prose.

JA: I think that has something to do with Amitabh's singing. [*both laugh*]

NMK: When you wrote 'Dekha ek khwaab', did the film already have the title? Or did your song inspire the title, *Silsila*?

JA: No, the title had already been chosen. So I intentionally used that word in the song. The hero, a poet, is in love with the heroine and the song is a celebration of their love. There were no complications at that stage of their relationship in the film. It was love without obstacles. It was a purely romantic song, though it paid attention to the surroundings in which it is sung—hence the reference to the flowers, etc., because Yash Chopra was to film it among the tulips in Holland.

NMK: How did you feel when you heard your first song recorded?

JA: Somehow I missed the actual recording. But I met Yash Chopra and his team the next day and heard the recorded song. It was a strange experience because generally you write dialogue first, then the film is shot, and you get to hear the dialogue spoken on the screen after many months. This was instant.

NMK: Since *Silsila*, you have written virtually hundreds of songs. Can you tell me how you go about writing a song? Who contacts you? You're sitting at home, the phone rings…

JA: Sometimes it's the producer or the composer who will call me. Say Anu Malik calls me and says, 'There's such and such director and he has come to me and I'm doing the music and he wants you to write the lyrics and so on. Would you like to do his film?' If I like the director or the proposal, I'll agree. Then we meet the director and he narrates the story in a nutshell and explains the situation in which the songs will feature in the narrative.

Then I'll write the lyrics and give them to the music director who composes a tune. We meet the film director and the composer will play five or six tunes and the director selects one. Or I might tell the composer, 'The other day you played me a tune which would be very good for this situation.' So we come to some conclusion.

It can also happen that Anu and I, or Jatin-Lalit and I, are sitting together and I think of some line and they make the tune right then and there. So when a director comes to us, I might suggest that we play him the song that we have in case he likes it.

NMK: What is your preferred method? Writing lyrics first or writing to a tune?

JA: It depends. If I like the tune, then it is a pleasure finding words for it. If one is not too happy with the tune, then it becomes slightly tedious for me.

Writing to the tune is a kind of art in itself—it's very tricky. It's not enough to get the words right—you have to understand the mood of the tune, the curves, the contours, so the words blend smoothly with them. You should feel this word was made for this musical note.

Majrooh Sahib is supposed to be *the* expert in this art. Some very well-known poets—I would not like to name them—have come to Bombay and have been given a chance to write film lyrics, but they could not write to the tune. Most poets write in the 12 or 13 familiar metres in Urdu and only understand those metres. Film tunes have all kinds of musical moods, and sometimes they are based on Latin American tunes or Western tunes. Let's say they're 'inspired' from certain sources so they have unusual metres—short metres where you have to make the words fit.

NMK: You mean when the tune has short musical phrases?

JA: Yes. So you have to understand these metres and have a musical ear. The tune has a certain temperament, a curvature, what you call 'meend'—gliding from one note to another. You must have an understanding and feel for it. Quite often the tune helps you because it defines what you can or cannot do.

NMK: You have worked with so many composers over the years—which experiences have stood out for you?

JA: Yes, I have worked with practically everyone. The ones who come to mind right now are R.D. Burman, Laxmikant-Pyarelal, Shiv-Hari, Rajesh Roshan, Anu Malik, A.R. Rahman, Shankar-Ehsaan-Loy, Jatin-Lalit, Bappi Lahiri, Bhupen Hazarika, Ismail Darbar, Adesh Srivastav, and Raju Singh. It goes without saying that they are all talented people, otherwise we would have never heard of them. They have all made a mark and continue to do so.

Working with these composers has had its own delights. It's strange—just as a person has two sides to their personality, it applies to art too. I feel that Anu Malik's strength is his tremendous wild energy as a musician and an almost obsessive passion for music. Working with Anu Malik is like trying to light a cigarette with a volcano. He puts that untamed energy into his music, but at the same time, it's a handicap because sometimes he tends to over-orchestrate the song, but whenever he holds back his orchestra and lets his composition take prominence, he gives great music.

If you hear Rajesh Roshan's music, you will hear a certain peaceful quality about it. He has a tremendous sense of rhythm, and every time you listen to his songs, you'll find a new beat, a new rhythm. There's something very sophisticated and gentle about his music, which is perhaps inherited from his illustrious father, the late Roshan. Rajesh Roshan's music always gives you a feeling that he's at peace with himself. But again, there's a danger that sometimes his music is too slow. The energy level decreases because it's so relaxed.

Take that very famous song that we did together, 'Ghar se nikalte hi' [As I stepped out of my house...]. —There's no hurry in that. There is no desperation, no anxiety of wondering: 'Will they listen to this song?' Nowadays when you hear a song, you sense that the people who have composed it don't have enough confidence, and think that if they don't increase the tempo, people won't listen. Rajesh Roshan does not have that kind of anxiety.

Then there is Jatin-Lalit; they are close in their musical style to R.D. Burman. Their melodies are tremendously sweet and intricate. They come from a family of musicians; their father is a great musician who teaches music and their uncle is the famous Pandit Jasraj. I have done a number of films with Jatin-Lalit.

NMK: You have also worked a lot with Shankar-Ehsaan-Loy. What was that experience like?

JA: These three young men make a formidable team. Together, they cover the complete spectrum of music from

Hindustani classical and Carnatic to Latin American, African, and Western classical. Their music varies from film to film. I think they also carry forward the best of R.D. Burman's style.

R.D. Burman is one of the finest music directors I've worked with. He has composed some extremely good music and some indifferent work, but it was never cheap or vulgar, or pedestrian. There is always complexity in his music, whether it is good or bad.

The last time we worked together was for *1942, A Love Story*, which was a very big musical hit. There were five songs in the film: three were written to the tune —'Ek ladki ko dekha to aisa laga' [I saw a girl that reminded me of ...], 'Kuchh na kaho' [Don't say a word] and 'Ye safar hai bahut kathin' [This journey is full of trials]. Then I gave R.D. Burman the lyrics of 'Rim jhim' [the pitter-patter of the falling rain] and 'Rooth na jaana' [Don't be upset] and he composed the tunes. 'Ek ladki ko dekha' had both male and female versions.

That was the leanest period in R.D.'s career; his back was against the wall. He had no work. Even the people closest to him had written him off. Hats off to Vinod Chopra that he put his faith in R.D. My career as a lyricist really took off after *1942, A Love Story* [released in 1994].

NMK: I am curious to know how you first came to work with R.D. Burman.

JA: After *Silsila*—that must have been in 1979–80, it's years ago now! How time flies! I did a very small film with a new music director called Kuldeep Singh. The film was *Saath Saath*. Jagjit Singh sang the songs. They were very big hits and are still played. In the 1980s and 1990s, HMV made many 'combination cassettes'—songs from two or three films on the same cassette, and *Saath Saath* and *Arth* was apparently the highest-selling cassette in HMV's history.

After *Saath Saath*, there were a few more films and then came *Saagar*—that was when I first worked with R.D. Burman.

NMK: What about A.R. Rahman?

JA: Rahman is an altogether different person. His language, his approach to a tune and a song situation, is different. The way he composes a tune, orchestrates, and records a song is totally unlike the others. He's from another planet. These days, I have noticed that he has developed a strange style of making a tune. What's his name, the man who wrote *A Brief History of Time?*

NMK: Stephen Hawking.

JA: Stephen Hawking doesn't know how the first atom came into existence, but after that point, he knows everything.

In the same way, I can't tell you *how* Rahman decides on a particular refrain. But he finds it, sits at his synthesizer, and keeps on improvising, and if he reaches a dead end, he goes back to the original refrain and gets into another groove. He records this improvisation and then chooses the phrases he likes— and that's how he makes a song. Rahman *lives* music.

Once we were talking and Rahman said, 'You know this tune has a certain mystical quality and the words should not be very definite, they should have an enigmatic feel.' I don't expect many music directors to talk about an 'enigmatic feel'.

Rahman also has a tremendous knowledge and understanding of music. His father was a music director, and I think Rahman was eight or nine years old when he started performing in public. Before he became a composer, he was among the finest keyboard players in the south.

NMK: Rahman's music sounds very Middle Eastern. He seems to have a lot of Egyptian influence, especially in the use of the violin—the style isn't very Indian.

JA: Generally his tunes *are* very Indian. [*starts humming a song from* Roja] When I sing the tune like this, it sounds purely Indian. I think generally his basic tunes are based on folk music or raags. It is in his orchestration that you hear other influences.

I believe that if you can write to a melody by Rahman, you can write to any tune. In most film songs, there's the mukhda, the returning refrain, and there are antaras—two or three stanzas that come in between the main refrain. Generally it is believed that the mukhda should be short and the antara should be longer.

Rahman is oblivious of any such rules and never adheres to them. I have written songs for him in which the mukhda has 12 lines and the antara has three lines—one example is the *Sapnay* song, 'Aawaara bhanware' [The wandering bees]. His approach to a song is totally different, so his tunes can go any which way. Perhaps that's the secret of Rahman's magic.

NMK: Tell me what do you think of his choice of playback singers—it's quite unusual.

JA: He has unusual choices. There are so many songs recorded by singers who have never sung before and will never sing again. A totally new girl sang that super-hit song 'Chinna chinna aasai' [This heart of mine has a little wish; 'Chhoti si aasha' in Hindi].

He believes in finding new voices because I think somewhere he thinks that if you keep recording the same voice, the song starts sounding old. So he experiments with voices much more than any other music director.

NMK: It also seems that he's the first Indian composer who keeps the words in the background and foregrounds the music. Some of the lyrics in P.K. Mishra's songs written for Rahman are difficult to make out. Take the title song in *Humse hai Muqabla*.

JA: Are you suggesting that Rahman doesn't let people know what P.K. Mishra has written? That makes Rahman P.K. Mishra's friend! [*laughs wholeheartedly*]

I understand what you are saying. Personally I don't have this complaint. It doesn't apply to my songs that he has composed.

But P.K. Mishra must have probably faced similar problems to the ones I did when writing for *Jeans*.

NMK: What were those problems?

JA: It was an interesting experience for me. A producer from south India, Dr Murli, who made the Tamil film *Jeans*, contacted me. The film was ready and the songs were written in Tamil and picturized. Now they were dubbing the picture in Hindi. The producer was rather apologetic and said, 'You may think it's below your dignity to do a dubbed film, but it's a good film—just see how the songs are picturized. We want you to write the songs for the Hindi version.'

The songs were so well picturized that I was tempted to do the work. Now I had to take three things into account: the song situation, the tune, and the lip-sync. In this process, I realized why the word 'problem' is called 'problem'—because it has 'p', 'b', and 'm'. In these three letters the lips meet. In so many lines, I had to make sure the lip movement of the Hindi/Urdu matched the Tamil words.

There's a situation in the picture where two boys and a girl take their grandmother to Las Vegas and Disneyland. The grandmother is a very happy-go-lucky old lady and she is dancing with them on the streets and so on. They sing a song for her. So at first I wrote:

Sab ki ho daadi, sab ki seheli
Kitni ho tum meethi
Aao na daadi hum naache gaayen
Aur tum bajaao seeti

[You're everyone's granny, a friend to all
How sweet you are
Granny, let's sing and dance
And you whistle a tune for us]

The producers said, 'This is not possible because the words won't match the lip-sync of the Tamil version.' So I rewrote:

Kehne ko daadi lekin seheli
Daadi ho to aisi
Sang sang ye naache
Sang sang ye naache
Sang sang ye gaaye, dekho to hai kaisi!
[She may be a granny, but she's a friend
That how grannies should be
She dances with us (x2)
She sings with us
See what a fun granny she is]

NMK: What do you think of fusion music? Is this a new trend?

JA: I don't think so. It amuses me when I hear people speak of fusion music as though it were something so new, so modern, and so contemporary. In fact, it's almost as old as Indian film music itself. What were the songs of the past maestros like R.C. Boral and Pankaj Mullick, if not fusion?

Take Pankaj Mullick's song 'Yaad aaye ki na aaye tumhaari' [Whether you miss me or not] or 'Pia milan ko jaana' [Do not forget to meet your beloved] from the film *Kapaal Kundal*, or his non-film song 'Praan chaahe nain na chaahe' [The soul desires, the eyes hesitate]. You have a generous use of Western instruments such as the piano, violin, trumpet, and Western percussions, while the tunes of these songs were very Indian. The song 'Praan chaahe nain na chaahe' is based on Raag Bilawal. The interlude music is, in fact, played on the piano.

Mera Saaya's song, composed by Madan Mohan, 'Tu jahaan jahaan chalega mera saaya saath hoga' [Wherever you may go, my shadow will follow you] is pure Raag Nand, and yet the music is totally symphonic. That was true fusion. The composers of the past were using Western musical language and blending it with Indian folk or classical music. But when we became estranged from our own musical traditions, what was left was not fusion but indeed confusion. [*both laugh*]

NMK: Of the older generation, which composer would you have liked to have worked with—Naushad, Shankar-Jaikishen, or S.D. Burman?

JA: [*replies immediately*] S.D. Burman. Shankar-Jaikishen have given such wonderful music, so have Naushad, Roshan, Madan Mohan, and many others. I don't like choosing one composer, but if I had to, it would be S.D. Burman. I have great respect for him. He had a rare sensitivity. S.D. Burman had a quality that you might call 'minimalist'. With very limited music, with very limited strokes, very delicately, he would create a tune. Generally, he did not have heavy orchestration—he did not use a 100-piece orchestra. His range was unbelievable. To think it's the same man who composed for *Chalti ka Naam Gaadi* and *Sujata*. There was tremendous complexity in S.D. Burman's music. In many ways, he was a composer who did not have a definite style. He would change his style according to the mood of the picture.

Right from my childhood, there were two people in the music world—besides Sahir—who were my favourites, S.D. Burman and Kishore Kumar. Even as a kid, in the days when Kishore Kumar used to sing only four or five songs a year, I'd prefer him to any other singer. Although that was the time when Rafi was king. Rafi was a great singer—what range he had! Not that I don't like him; I have great respect for

Mohammed Rafi—maybe it's a Sophie's Choice, but I'd say Kishore's voice appealed to me the most. His voice became very popular when Indian society began to accept a kind of Western sophistication.

Before A.R. Rahman, in fact, S.D. Burman occasionally broke the classical structure of the song and composed certain songs in which there was no difference between the mukhda and the antara, or the whole song was composed as one piece, like 'Dil ek shaayar hai' [The heart is a poet], sung by Kishore Kumar and written by Neeraj in *The Gambler*.

A song by Kaifi Azmi did the same in a Madan Mohan composition from *Haqeeqat*, 'Main ye soch kar uske dar se utha tha' [I left her doorway with this thought in mind]—this song doesn't have a mukhda or antara. Its structure is closer to a nazm [poem] than to a geet [lyric/song].

I once wrote a song in *Saagar* that Lata Mangeshkar sang—the sad version of 'Saagar kinaare' [On the seashore]. It starts with an antara, and as the song ends, we go to the mukhda.

But these songs are exceptions. Somehow we feel more secure with a mukhda because it is repeated and so enters people's memory. If you have a song without a hook line, then nothing will be repeated and people may not necessarily remember the words.

The other thing is that most Indian film songs have been unable to cut their umbilical cord with the ghazal and the folk song. Folk songs like film songs have mukhdas and antaras. We now call the main refrain the 'hook line', but what difference does it make what we call it? The fact remains that poetically the structure of the film song mirrors the Indian folk song.

NMK: What must you always keep in mind when writing a song?

JA: When writing, you have to respect the intelligence and sensitivity of the listener and leave something to their imagination. It will not work if you try to state everything, because the reader or listener cannot participate. You have left no room for involvement. It is only when a person can imagine and contribute his or her emotions and experiences to those lines that the expression is completed. Subtlety is desirable in poetry, but there are many who write absurdity in the guise of symbolism. I have no patience for such fraudsters.

NMK: You said a script does not necessarily come to you in a linear order—is it the same way you write a song?

JA: No, I write from start to finish. I try to give a definite structure to my songs. First of all, I think of an angle or theme. There are usually seven or eight song situations in a film, and you have to write for those situations again and again and again. So each time there has to be something new and fresh. So the moment I decide on the angle, I write the first two lines. Generally the antaras have nothing to do with each other. They talk of different things. But I don't do that. When I find a theme, I try to make sure that the whole song says the same thing, so there is a sense of completion at the end. Unconsciously, I have taken this structure from Sahir Ludhianvi's writing.

NMK: Do you try to keep the song close to a poem in terms of its metre?

JA: I can't decide the metre if I am writing to a tune. There are musical notes that require words with a certain weight. [*hums the tune of* 'Kuchh na kaho'] If I had written 'Qayaamat hai' [The end of the world] on this tune, it would not have sounded good even if the words were in the right metre. The notes are delicate and light.

For certain tunes, you need stronger words. [*hums a marching tune*] If you place light words on a tune like this, they'll fly off. The words must sit on the beat. [*hums the opening bars of the* Mr India *song,* 'Kaatey nahin kat'te ye din ye raat'[These days, these nights never end]. The words in this song suit the tune, but if I had written, 'Haule se tum jo aaye to ye...' [Softly you entered], it would not have sounded right. The mukhda and the antaras must work together.

NMK: In the *Virasat* song, 'Dhol bajne laga' [The drums start to play], sung by Udit Narayan, I particularly liked the stanza that starts with 'Mohabbat se bhara' [A heart full of love].

JA: Thank you very much. Do you know something—I'm so proud of those lines! And you're the first person who has remarked on them. Until today, no one has talked to me about them. [*he quotes the lines*]

Mohabbat se bhara ek dil hai jaise
Mere bachpan ka saathi mera gaon
Bahut meetha hai paani is kunwe ka
Bahut thandi hai in pairon ki chhaon
Ghula sangeet hai jaise hawa mein
Zara aawaaz to sun chakkiyon ki
Rehat gaata hai dheeme-dheeme sur mein
Sureeli boliyaan hain panchhiyon ki
Main barson baad lauta hoon to jaana
Ye gaaon geet hai sadiyon puraana
[Like a heart filled with love
My childhood friend, my village
So sweet is the water from this well
So cool is the shade of these trees
Music seems to waft in the breeze
Listen to the rhythm of the grinding stone
The water wheel sings in soft notes
The birds sing melodious tunes

I return after many long years to discover
My village is a song, centuries old]

NMK: The *Mr India* songs had such fresh energy. Take the opening lines in 'Hawa Hawaai'—the idea that you can use nonsensical words, like the old number 'Eena meena deeka', is an interesting way to start a song.

JA: I wrote the script for *Mr India*. There was a scene in the film where the heroine, Sridevi, pretends to be a cabaret dancer from Havana, and calls herself 'Miss Hawa Hawaai from Havana'.

In Urdu, we have an expression, we say, 'Bhai, kahaan hawa hawaai ghoom rahe ho?' [Brother, why are you rushing about?] It's a UP expression. The sound of 'Hawa Hawaai' was rather interesting. So when I wrote the song for this situation, I used the name in the song, 'Kehte hain mujh ko Hawa Hawaai' [They call me Hawa Hawaai].

Do you know when *Mr India* and *Tezaab* were released, these two top heroines, Sridevi and Madhuri Dixit, who were competing with each other, were branded by the media as Miss Hawa Hawaai and the Ek Do Teen girl?

NMK: Yes. I have heard that. What's interesting is that the words sound so modern that few would guess they're an old UP expression. [*JA smiles*] I always thought they referred to Hawaii.

JA: Miss Hawa Hawaai from Havana.

NMK: It sounds like a character name you might have found in the work of your favourite writer, Ibn-e-Safi.

JA: Yes!

NMK: When you write a song, how do you know the song is as good as it can be?

JA: A feeling needs to be articulated, and you know if you have not quite got it. Then comes along a line and you think, 'Ah! This is it!' After all, you're trying to feel and identify with emotions that must come from the depth of your heart. Sometimes it happens instantly, and sometimes you have to delve deeper. One may create a song that's good enough but does not have that killer line.

There was a situation in the film *Saagar* in which one of the heroes, played by Kamal Haasan, has lost the love of his life to a rival. He sings a song at the engagement party of his beloved, who now loves someone else, and in that song is this stanza:

Sach mere yaar hai
Bas vohi pyaar hai
Jis ke badle mein koi to pyaar de
Baaqi bekaar hai
[It's true, my friend
Only that love is true
If it wins love in return
All else is meaningless]

Now there's a stanza that goes like this:

Samjhe the hum ye zindagi gham
aur khushi ka mel hai
Hum ko magar aaya nazar ye zindagi vo khel hai
Koi sab jeete sab koi haar de
Apni to haar hai
[I thought life was both sadness and joy
But I can see life is a kind of game
Some win it all, some lose it all
Loss is clearly my share]

When I wrote the last line, I thought it might touch people. It's a simple statement, no art, and no intricacy—simple and definite. It needed the weight of the preceding words, but a line like that completed the thought.

NMK: In terms of your own involvement in a song, are you more yourself when writing a sad or a happy song?

JA: I think this is not only true of me, but of most writers. When a writer or poet is writing about sadness, he must delve into his psyche. Sad moments and experiences usually settle deep within a person. So you must dig deeper. Similar feelings are hidden deep in people who will hear the song, and so sad songs connect to their inner world. That's why poignant songs and moving poetry have greater and longer lasting impact. Sadness often finds expression in songs.

NMK: Would you agree that this kind of hidden sadness runs through your title song in the film *Kal Ho Na Ho* [Tomorrow may never come]?

JA: Yes.

Main hoon sar ko jhukaaye
Tum ho gham ko chupaaye
Tum bhi chup ho
Main bhi chup hoon
Kaun kise samjhaaye
Sach hai ki dil to dukha hai
Hum ne magar socha hai
Dil ko hai gham kyun
Aankh hai nam kyun
Hona hi tha jo hua hai
[I stand with head hung low
While you hide all sorrow
You say nothing
I say nothing
How to console one another?
It's true that my heart is aching

But my mind is made up
Why is the heart so forlorn?
Why is the eye so moist?
What had to happen has happened]

When Shabana heard this song, she said, 'This is typically you.
The way you understate hurt or sorrow in your life and in your
poetry.' Maybe she is right because I believe if you wallow in
self-pity, others do not feel the need to cry. You only humiliate
yourself and disgust others.

NMK: The character that Amitabh Bachchan has played in so
many of the films co-written by you is of a person who hates
being a victim, psychologically or socially, and is too proud
to show any kind of emotional vulnerability. It seems holding
pain back revisits your work in many forms, including in
your songs.

JA: What touches me the most in films, literature, or poetry
are characters who find themselves in adverse circumstances but
maintain their dignity and never beg for pity. When a person
is in deep pain and you can see they are trying to fight that
pain, you respect them for maintaining their dignity in a
difficult situation.

NMK: I wonder whether your childhood experiences made you
repress your feelings, preferring silence to expressing feelings.

JA: You will have to call my brother, Dr Salman Akhtar, who's
a psychoanalyst, as I have mentioned, and he can answer this
question. [both laugh] By the way, he is an excellent poet, too.

NMK: Knowing what you know today of songwriting, if
you could interview the great lyricists of the past now—what
would you ask?

JA: That depends on which lyricist I am interviewing. I'd ask
different kinds of questions to Sahir and others to Shailendra.

I've noticed that Sahir had a very interesting structure in many of his romantic songs. One line talks of the abstract nature of beauty and the surroundings, while the next line is about the beloved and alludes to her sensuality.

Take the lines:

Pedon ki shaakhon pe soyi soyi chaandni
Tere khayaalon mein khoyi khoyi chaandni
Aur thodi der mein thak ke laut jaayegi
Raat ye bahaar ki phir kabhi na aayegi
[Slumbering moonlight drapes the tree branches
Wistful moonlight fills your thoughts
Soon it will tire and fade away
This spring night will never return again]

Sahir never allows you to forget the surroundings, the backdrop, but he constantly juxtaposes the beauty of nature with his love for a woman. So the song develops a certain mystical and aesthetic quality—yet it does not become totally abstract because the woman and her physicality are constantly present. In this way, perhaps Sahir is seeking distraction from the predictability of the romantic song. I would ask him if he did this intentionally.

NMK: I wonder if Sahir's approach to the song can find an equivalence in cinema language between say the wide shot and the close-up. In the same example of Guru Dutt's *Jaal* song 'Ye raat ye chaandni', wide shots of palm trees swaying in the night breeze are cut together with close-ups of the heroine. The bigger picture and the detail are juxtaposed.

JA: If the song offers a synthesis between the couple's passion and the beauty of nature, it does allow for close-ups and wide shots, but ultimately this depends on the sensitivity and cinematic language of the film director.

NMK: Bearing mind how dependent song picturization is about 'showing' the beauty of nature, do you think Sahir deliberately wrote of nature? Do you think Sahir's lines came first or the director's idea about how he planned to film the song?

JA: It is usually the director who determines the setting and then the lyrics follow. But sometimes it is indeed the lyrics that give the director ideas. So maybe Sahir's songs provided the visuals, but what is more appreciable is that this play between the beloved and nature make passion ethereal. It adds a certain aura, a sense of purity, and a larger-than-life quality. The song is greater than if it were only talking about you and me, him and her, or whatever. This love between the man and woman becomes the dance of the universe.

NMK: You met Sahir Ludhianvi many times; did you think of asking him, for example, why he used nature in his songs in the way that he did?

JA: I never thought of it at that time. I was not even aware of it myself. But I do know that Sahir found different ways of looking at romance and did not always depend on nature. Take the song, 'Tum agar mujhko na chaaho to koi baat nahin, tum kisi aur ko chaahogi to mushkil hogi' [It matters little if you do not desire me, but if you desire another, that would be a problem] from *Dil Hi to Hai*. Here he is on new ground. He does not need nature's help.

NMK: Did you think Sahir was interested in nature?

JA: Ye aap kabhi khayaal bhi mat ki jiyega [Never let such a thought even cross your mind]! Poets are very strange people—their sources are strange. You can never tell from where they draw their inspiration. I think they store things away. Whatever they have seen many years before enters their memory and can be recalled at any time. So while the poet is sitting on a hot afternoon in a closed room, he writes about a 'chaandni raat' [a moonlit night].

There is a difference between a poet and a reporter. The reporter has to *be* in a chaandni raat to report it. [*NMK laughs*]

The poet doesn't have that problem. If he has seen a full moon ten years earlier, he can describe it on some humid and balmy afternoon.

NMK: What else did you notice in Sahir's songwriting?

JA: In a Sahir song, the theme remains constant in each stanza. He adorns, embellishes, and develops the same idea all through the song. You can see this approach in 'Zindagi bhar nahin bhoolegi vo barsaat ki raat' [All my life, never shall I forget that rainy night] from *Barsaat ki Raat*, 'Abhi na jaao chhod kar ki dil abhi bhara nahin' [Do not leave me now and go. My heart has not had its fill of you] from *Hum Dono*, and 'Maine shaayed tumhen pehele bhi kahin dekha hai' [I think I have seen you somewhere before], again from *Barsaat ki Raat*. He establishes a particular angle in the song and is loyal to it throughout the song—this is close to how a nazm works.

NMK: Sahir was famous for his poetry, but did he enjoy writing film songs?

JA: Sahir took it very seriously. But he wrote them on his own terms. He was the first person who brought the film song closer to the poem. Think of 'Vo subah kabhi to aayegi' [The new dawn will break some day] or the songs in *Pyaasa*—they are like poems. Sahir has written lyrics too, but he made his mark because of the poems that he wrote for films.

As an Urdu poet, Sahir had developed such a fine sense of phonetics, and when he wrote in Hindi, he applied the same sensitivity. In the same light, I don't think many Hindi writers could write dialogue like the dialogue that Dr Rahi Masoom Raza wrote for the television series *Mahabharat*.

Now think of Sahir's Hindi songs like 'Aaj sajan mohe ang laga lo' [Hold me in your arms today, my beloved], or the *Chitralekha* song, 'Mann re tu kaahe na dheer dhare?' [O heart, why must you be so uneasy?] You see a poet at work, not a lyricist:

Mann re tu kaahe na dheer dhare
Vo nirmohi moh na jaane jinka moh kare
Utna hi upkaar samajh koi jitna saath nibha de
Janam maran ka mel hai sapna
Ye sapna bisra de
Koi na sang mare
[O heart, why be disheartened?
The one you feel for has no feelings
Be grateful for the time spent together
Togetherness until death is a dream
Forget this dream
When you die, you die alone]

NMK: Did you get the sense that Sahir was very aware of his contribution to poetry?

JA: Oh yes. I spent many evenings with him. We had long conversations. I knew him very well. He was an extremely proud person. I don't want to use the word 'arrogant' [*laughs*], but humility was not one of his virtues.

There is something charismatic about Sahir's poetry. Even today, he is one of the most popular Urdu poets. The critics do not accept him as a great poet at all—they don't include him with the great poets. But you cannot challenge his popularity as an Urdu poet and lyricist. He elevated the film song hugely. Urdu poets have that strong tradition of Urdu poetry behind them, so however simply they wrote, they had that tradition to fall back on. Sahir's literary background was always present in his film songs.

NMK: What about the expression in folk poetry?

JA: If you're looking for that kind of poetic expression, you'll find it in the work of Nazeer Akbarabadi. For example, he will say, 'Sab thaat pada reh jaayega jab laad chalega banjaara' [All grandeur and riches will be left far behind when the wanderer makes his way]. Nazeer used symbols belonging to the folk tradition in the way that he described life.

During his lifetime, Nazeer was not recognized by Urdu historians or critics. He was a contemporary of Mir, who was considered a great poet. Mir also wrote on Urdu poetry but never mentioned Nazeer. A barefooted poet, Nazeer travelled from town to town, village to village. He would go to village fairs and write poetry about a watermelon, a jug, or a pitcher. He has written many poems on Holi and Diwali and on village festivals. Kabir's influence on Nazeer is clear. Like Kabir says:

Chori kare nihai ki, karain sui ka daan
Upar chadh kar dekhat hain, kekat door vimaan
[Stealing the blacksmith's anvil, donating a needle
Rushing to the roof terrace, awaiting a heavenly chariot]

Now a traditional Urdu poet will not use such imagery. But these symbols are real, and they touch you because they're real. I must add that Urdu by temperament is an extremely urbane language. The court and the aristocracy patronized it. For over 300 years, writers and poets have worked on Urdu phonetics, and have rejected words that are not pleasant to hear. They have shaped the language and the vocabulary to make Urdu into a very sophisticated language, so the expression has that blue-blooded quality. There is something aristocratic about Urdu however humble it may try to be.

NMK: Can we talk about Shailendra? What were his qualities? Had you met him?

JA: I did not know Shailendra personally. I would say his language was much simpler and lighter than Sahir's. Shailendra's songs remind you of songs that have been sung for hundreds of years in Indian villages and towns.

His style was closer to that of the poet Nazeer. Kabir and Mir also influenced him. You'll find a touch of Sufism and folk wisdom in his lyrics. Look at the song in the film *Guide*, 'Wahan kaun hai tera, musafir, jaayega kahan?' [Who can you call your own, O Traveller, where will you go?], and you'll see how close he is to Kabir or Rahim:

> Tu ne to sab ko raah dikhaayi
> Tu apni manzil kyun bhoola
> Auron ki uljhan suljha ke raaja
> Kyun kachche dhaagon mein jhoola?
> Kyun naache sapera?
> [You showed the way to one and all
> Why did you forget your own destination?
> Untying the knotted lives of others
> Why entangle yourself in unspun thread?
> Why does the snake charmer dance?]

Shailendra was a master of saying something very emotional and deep in ordinary and simple words. He wrote in both Hindi and Urdu, and the kind of Hindi he used was unlike that of many other Hindi writers. There was gentleness, softness, and warmth. Hindi writers sometimes tend to use Sanskritized Hindi that sounds phonetically harsh.

Majrooh Sahib once told me that he and his contemporaries were poets who wrote lyrics, but Shailendra was a lyricist in the true sense of the word. Shailendra was also political and involved with IPTA [Indian Peoples' Theatre Association—an off-shoot of the Communist Party of India]. You can sense his leftist leanings running through many songs, including songs like 'Dil ka haal sune dilwaala' [Only the big-hearted listen to the woes of others] from *Shree 420*:

Chhote se ghar mein ghareeb ka beta
Main bhi hoon ma ke naseeb ka beta
Ranj-o-gham bachpan ke saathi
Aandhiyon mein jali jeevan baati
Bhook ne hai bade pyaar se paala
Dil ka haal sune dilwaala
[I'm the son born into a poor family
My mother blessed her luck all the same
Anger and sorrow were childhood friends
My life's flame braved many storms
Hunger nurtured me with great affection
Only the large-hearted listen to the woes of others]

Shailendra had that kind of velvety quality that was deeply rooted in folk tradition. He brought that vocabulary, innocence, simplicity, and spontaneity to film songs. I can't think of many Hindi poets who have a better phonetic sense than Shailendra. Another fine example is the song 'Kaise din beete kaise beeti ratiyaan, pia jaane na' [How the days and nights passed, my beloved knows not] from *Anuradha*.

NMK: What do you think about Shakeel Badayuni's work?

JA: His craft and vocabulary were impeccable. Only someone from UP could have this kind of command over Hindustani diction. Most of his songs were written in collaboration with the composer Naushad, and perhaps because his reputation overshadowed that of Shakeel's, the latter did not get the recognition that he rightly deserved. Take the title song of 'Mere mehboob' [My beloved]—it's the words that hold the interest and impact of the song, not the tune. He was equally skilled in a song liked 'Mann tarpat' [My uneasy heart] from *Baiju Bawra*. This song shows Shakeel's versatility. But I suppose the last word in versatility belongs to Majrooh Sultanpuri, who had a water-like quality.

NMK: Yes! He wrote songs for *Chalti ka Naam Gaadi*, *Sujata*, and *Mamta*. He wrote 'Gham diye mustaqil' [Endless was the suffering inflicted] sung by K.L. Saigal in the 1940s' film *Shahjehan*, and then in 1988, he wrote 'Papa kehte hain bada naam karega' [Papa says you'll be famous one day] for *Qayamat se Qayamat Tak*. What extraordinary range!

JA: Majrooh Sahib survived as a successful songwriter for almost six decades during which time there was a huge change in aesthetics, diction, and language, and a radical change in the temperament of music. To sail through the passing years and yet remain relevant and contemporary is not easy. Many songwriters have come and drowned in the tides of time with beloveds like balma and sajna [*JA smiles*]. But Majrooh Sahib survived and kept reinventing himself.

I must tell you that Majrooh Sahib's poetry and songs have nothing to do with one another. His vocabulary and diction in the ghazal is Persianized and tradition bound. But when it comes to songwriting, the UP lad in Majrooh Sultanpuri suddenly wakes up and he becomes another person. Take 'Arre yaar meri tum bhi ho ghazab, ghunghat to zara odho' [My friend, you're stunning, you better cover yourself with a veil], a song that he wrote for *Teen Deviyan*.

NMK: What about Kaifi Azmi's songs?

JA: His body of work is much smaller than that of other songwriters. Although he wrote for a small number of films, he has written such excellent songs, including 'Waqt ne kiya kya haseen sitam' [Time has inflicted such sweet cruelty on us] for *Kaagaz ke Phool*, and 'Chalte chalte yunhi koi mil gaya tha' [As I was walking, I met someone by chance...] for *Pakeezah*.

By temperament, Kaifi Azmi was more of a poet than a lyricist. Take 'Bichhde sabhi baari baari' [They abandoned me one by one] in *Kaagaz ke Phool* or 'Ye duniya ye mehfil mere kaam ki nahin' [This world means nothing to me] from *Heer Ranjha*. He had the dignity and the power of a poet in his lyrics. He was not a regular professional lyricist like the others who churned out songs by the dozen.

NMK: Who is the most underrated lyricist to your mind?

JA: It is undoubtedly Anand Bakshi. When we speak of the great lyricists, we always refer to Sahir, Majrooh, Kaifi, and Shakeel—in part because they were considered poets in their own right. When we speak of Shailendra, we quickly add how he was associated with the Communist Party, the leftist movement, and IPTA. However, we have a certain snobbery about Anand Bakshi, who never had this intellectual halo. He has written over 3,000 songs and had cornered the market from the 1970s. Perhaps he should figure in the *Guinness Book of Records* as the most prolific lyricist in the world. If we look at his work, his songs show tremendous range. Of course, many of his songs don't go beyond the mediocre, but he has also written scores of great songs. For example, take his work in *Amar Prem* or *Milan*. One of my all-time favourites is his 'Zindagi ke safar mein guzar jaate hain jo muqaam, vo phir nahin aate' [On the journey of life, the moments you live will never return] from *Aap ki Kasam*.

My father Jaan Nisar Akhtar, Rajendra Krishen, Raja Mehdi Ali Khan, Anjaan, Bharat Vyas, H.S. Bihar, Shevan Rizvi—they have all written exceptionally good songs, but they did not have the individual stamp of Sahir and Shailendra. In all fairness, we must include the work of the poet Pradeep, who had a very individual style. These lyricists wrote wonderful songs, but no one talks about them. They did good work and were very competent. But they have been largely forgotten. Take Vengsarkar—he was a very good cricketer, but people do not remember him in the same way they remember other cricketers who were not as consistent as Vengsarkar.

NMK: So it's not just a question of the quality of one's work?

JA: It's the whole thing, the whole aura. Think of the writer Vahajat Mirza. Who talks about him now? How many people know who he is? I mean this is the man who wrote the dialogue for *Mughal-e-Azam*, *Gunga Jumna*, and *Mother India*. Oh my God! But no one mentions him. What a great writer he was! It has something to do with personal charisma, the whole persona, or how the person is presented.

NMK: Coming back to songs, which lyricist was a model for your songwriting?

JA: I have admired almost all the lyricists of the 1950s and 1960s, but, as you know, I have particular regard for Sahir, Shailendra, Majrooh, and Kaifi. With all due respect, however, I'm afraid I don't have a model. All good writing has influenced me in one way or another. I have been influenced by classical poetry and folk literature as well. One learns from many sources, but ultimately one must find one's own voice. The work must come from one's own experience, sensitivity, and aesthetics; otherwise it will end up sounding fake and a poor imitation.

NMK: I wonder if there is evidence of good songwriting nowadays ...

JA: Take Sameer. He has taken the place once occupied by Anand Bakshi. He's prolific to an amazing extent. We also have Gulzar, who is known for his tremendous sense of phonetics and unusual choice of words. His style is so different and easily identifiable. In recent years, many of his songs have been chartbusters, including 'Chhaiyyaan chhaiyyaan' [In the shade of love] from *Dil Se*, 'Beedi jalaale' [Light your 'beedi'] from *Omkara*, and 'Chappa-chappa' [The wheel turns] from *Maachis*.

Among the newcomers, Prasoon Joshi, Ajay Jhingran, Irshad Kamil, Swanand Kirkire, and Kausar Munir show a lot of promise.

NMK: Does a lyricist have to be a great poet?

JA: No, he doesn't, but he must be versatile and know how to write to music. If you're writing to the tune, you have to work in unusual metres, not only regular metres. Sometimes you need to write a lullaby, a mujra, a qawwali, a bhajan, or a cabaret song. So you must have adequate expression and vocabulary at your command. If you are to write a qawwali, you will have to know Sufi poetry and the kinds of qawwali that already exist. The same applies to a bhajan—you must know its metaphors and symbols. These skills will only be at hand when you have read a lot of poetry. It takes time. No shortcuts, no crash course is possible. It's not difficult to write two lines in metre, but quite often people make mistakes even in those two lines because they are not trained. You should never be short of words, phrases, or metaphors. There is a word in music called taiyyaari [preparation]; the same applies to poetry and lyric writing.

NMK: This sort of lack of training or preparation seems to be prevalent in many professions. It's the way of the world now.

JA: It applies to music too. Someone sings a little, or studies music for three months and thinks he or she can become a playback singer. Can you become a Lata Mangeshkar? You cannot. Lata Mangeshkar chose to be a playback singer. But if that same lady had decided to become a classical singer, she would have been a challenge to any classical singer.

At the outset, I have to say Lata Mangeshkar is to playback singing what Shakespeare is to literature; Rafi is what Michelangelo is to sculpture; Kishore Kumar is what Thomas Edison is to invention.

Lata Mangeshkar's grounding in music is so solid. When I started writing lyrics, she had stopped singing on a regular basis, and so she sang only about 15 of my songs. How flawlessly she sang the sad version of 'Saagar kinaare' and 'Ye kahaan aa gaye hum' in *Silsila*. There's a line in the song, 'Hui aur bhi mulaayam meri shaam dhalte-dhalte' [The evening became even softer as it was fading]. I really wonder whether any singer in the world could sing the word 'mulaayam' [soft] more meaningfully than Lata Mangeshkar.

Listen to how she sang the theme song 'Maati re maati' [Mere illusions] in the film *The Godmother*. Listen to the line 'Thak gayin hoon ladte-ladte apne jeevan se' [I am tired of a life of conflict].

Can you become an Asha Bhosle without having significant grounding? She is like Menaka.

Let me tell you Menaka's story. There was once a great sage, Vishwamitra, who through penance and mediation was becoming as powerful as the gods. The gods were displeased and decided to send to earth an apsara [heavenly being] called Menaka to distract the sage. With her alluring and seductive manner, she succeeded in distracting the concentration of even the great Vishwamitra. The only difference between Asha Bhosle and Menaka is that Menaka danced, while Asha Bhonsle sings.

Lata, Rafi, Asha Bhosle, and Kishore Kumar were masters. So when they sang a film song, it felt as easy as pie. They had swallowed oceans of music, and singing a film song required them to shower a few drops. Thank God, we still have Lata Mangeshkar and Asha Bhosle.

There were other singers too, like Mukesh, Talat Mahmood, Manna Dey, Shamshad Begum, Geeta Dutt, Hemant Kumar—they were not just singers but in their own right, they have become representative of different genres of singing.

NMK: What about the generation that rose to prominence in the 2000s?

JA: It really isn't fair to compare the new generation of playback singers to the all-time greats. Nevertheless, we have exceptionally talented singers like Alka Yagnik, who has an ethereal voice. There's Sonu Nigam and Udit Narayan, who has a totally original timbre. They are doing extremely well. We have Hariharan, who has a strong grounding in classical music. Shankar Mahadevan has chosen to be a music director, but he is also a great singer. I hope you have heard our non-film album *Breathless?* Not many singers can achieve what Shankar has managed to do in this album. To say the least, the songs would leave many a singer breathless!

NMK: When a singer is recording your song, do you change the words at the last minute?

JA: Yes! I'm known for that. I do it quite often. I write the song in a few hours. Then I keep changing it until it is recorded. A little word here and there is changed. Even when the singer is at the mic, I'll request him or her to change a certain word. So that adjustment goes on until the song is recorded. If I can, I prefer attending the recording.

Many playback singers have very good voices and know about music, but they do not all have Hindi or Urdu as their mother tongue. So it's handy if the lyricist is around when the song is being recorded. They may pronounce the words correctly but can stress the wrong word or syllable. Sometimes, in singing, you have to say a word quickly and stretch another. If there are four words in a line, the singers don't always know which word can be stretched and which should be sung short. What will sound better musically? So you have to guide them. Many singers will pronounce the word 'mohabbat' as 'mohubbat'. That's just a simple example.

With Ramesh Sippy and Dilip Kumar at Dilip Kumar's birthday party in his house, 1978.

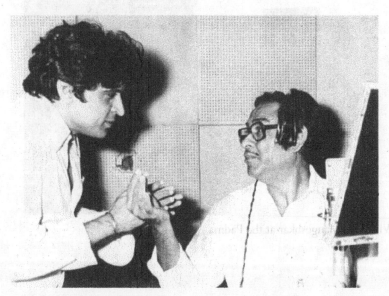

With Kishore Kumar at a song recording for *Saagar*, 1986.

With Lata Mangeshkar at the Padma Awards, 1999.

Flanked by Mehdi Hasan and Majrooh Sultanpuri at a party in Javed Akhtar's home, 1978.

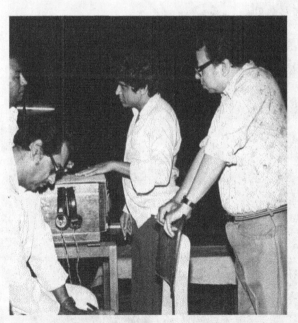

With Swapan Chakrabarti (left), Kishore Kumar, and R.D. Burman at a recording for *Saagar*, 1986.

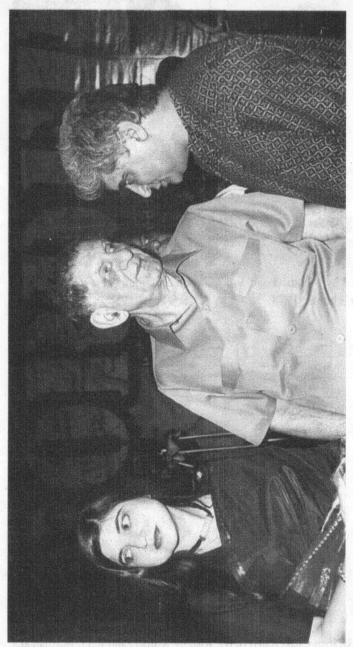

With Alka Yagnik and Anand Bakshi, 1997.

Javed Akhtar surrounded by fans at a school function in Ahmedabad, 2000.

With (left to right) Ehsaan, Loy, Shankar, and Nikhil Advani at a music sitting for *Kal Ho Na Ho*, 2001.

With Shah Rukh Khan on the sets of *Main Hoon Na*, 2004.
Photo: Peter Chappell.

Sharing a joke with Amitabh Bachchan as Naresh Goyal of Jet Airways and
Yash Chopra look on, at a function in 2003.

NMK: For people entirely unfamiliar with Hindi cinema, can you run through the kind of situations in which songs are used in a film?

JA: A lyricist may be asked to write a song on any kind of situation, but most often the demand is limited to romantic situations. Since these situations are predictable, you must introduce novelty in the song's vocabulary. I try to pick words that have not been previously used. Yet it is so ironic that filmmakers are extremely wary of new words.

If you look at the songs of the past ten years—and please leave my songs out [both laugh]—you will realize that Hindi film songs have imprisoned themselves in 40–50 words. 'Deewaana' [crazy lover], 'jaaneman' [my life], 'sanam' [beloved], or 'jaadu' [magic]—these sorts of words. As almost all songs are in some way or the other love songs, so the use of words like 'dil' [heart], 'pyaar' and 'mohabbat' [love] has become inevitable.

I do understand the problem that lyric writers face because they need to write songs for the same situations and do so repeatedly. Very rarely therefore do you hear a song with new words. And when such a song appears, you appreciate it. In the long run, that is not an excuse for writing clichéd songs. Despite the constraints, we must always try to find an original angle, a new thought, and a fresh metaphor.

NMK: Beyond the vocabulary and the thought, the symbols are also repeated. I am thinking of the image of the moon.

JA: The symbol of the moon is almost as old as the moon itself. First of all, the moon is beautiful. It exudes a feeling of peace and serenity. Moonlight is not harsh but soft, and wherever it falls, it makes everything look romantic.

I agree when such symbols are overused, you get desensitized. If your heart is touched at the same place repeatedly, it tends to develop a kind of 'corn' there. But use the symbol of the moon with a new image laced around it, it sounds fine.

For example, I have used the metaphor of the moon in quite a few songs. In *Refugee*, there was a song, 'Raat ki hatheli par chaand jagmagaata hai' [On the palm of night, the moon shimmers]. The moon has become new in this instance because it is in the company of the 'palm of the night'—which is a different kind of imagery.

In *Sapnay*—a film by Rajeev Menon with music by A.R. Rahman—I wrote a song, 'Chanda re chanda re, kabhi to zameen pe aa, baithenge, baaten karenge' [O moon, won't you descend to earth? We could sit and chat]. No one makes such informal offers to the moon. Here, the words are treating the moon like a friend. That added a new touch.

There are also many expressions that were used in the 1940s and 1950s that have fallen away. Bringing a new sensibility to those words and metaphors makes them sound appealing. It's like placing an antique piece in a modern house. It stands out but looks charming.

NMK: I am curious about the connection between your words and the way the song will ultimately be filmed. How detailed a briefing does the film's director give you and the music director?

JA: Someone like Yash Chopra will tell you how he is going to picturize the song and in what location. As I mentioned earlier, he told me he would shoot the *Silsila* song in the tulip fields in Holland. That gave me an idea for the song. After many years, I once again wrote lyrics for Yash Chopra. I wrote a long song with many verses. Some verses were going to be filmed as a romantic montage, so Yash Chopra told me about the kind of locations he would use. Those visuals appear in my lyrics.

NMK: Have you ever gone to the cinema and been appalled by the way the song that you've written has been picturized?

JA: Many times. One writes a song with tremendous attention, taking care about every word. Suddenly you see the hero and the heroine in long shot—their faces are barely visible and so the actors cannot give expression to the words. They are merrily doing their aerobics whilst singing the song. They could be singing 'Jack and Jill' for all we know.

NMK: In the 1960s, the Shammi Kapoor era, dance was popular then too. I am wondering if people danced to Hindi film music at parties or clubs in those days as they do now.

JA: I don't think so. I believe the middle-class audiences of the 1950s and 1960s were far more prudish. Why only the audience? Even actors were not ready to start dancing at the drop of a hat. With the exception of Shammi Kapoor, who had his own exuberant dance style, most actors of that time would perform the song like a scene. If you see old movies, the hero and heroine would stand in one place and sing. If they moved at all, they would move like normal human beings. You can see the face of the person who is singing the song. Whether it was Dilip Kumar, Raj Kapoor, Meena Kumari, or Nargis, their singing on screen was conversational as though they were talking to the other person. Dance numbers are now a form of gymnastics. Mercifully, there are some recent song picturizations that belong to the realm of the sane.

NMK: The vast majority of songs are romantic. So in what situations would you use the different words in Hindi and Urdu for love such as, 'pyaar', 'ishq', and 'mohabbat'?

JA: These words have different cultural backgrounds and different weights. Obviously where the word 'pyaar' will fit in a line, 'ishq' would be too short. Where 'mohabbat' could work, 'pyaar' is too short. What's more important are the other words in the line. What is the mood of the song? What is the mukhda?

Suppose the song is a village song, I may use 'pyaar' or 'prem' and not 'mohabbat', which is a more urban word. But there is a difference between 'mohabbat' and 'ishq'. 'Mohabbat' is love within the realm of reason and has greater social sanction than 'ishq'. 'Mohabbat' is also used for the love of a mother, father, or sister. But when love becomes obsessive, you start calling it 'ishq'.

'Pyaar' is a more colloquial word. As a matter of fact, you might not find it in traditional Urdu poetry, but you will find the words 'ishq' and 'mohabbat'. Even today, the word 'pyaar' belongs more to films than to serious poetry.

NMK: What about words addressing the beloved?

JA: Most of them have become clichés like 'jaaneman' [my life], 'jaan-e-jaan' [life of my life]. I try to avoid them. There is another word 'sanam', which was introduced into film songs by none other than Majrooh Sultanpuri. He was the first person who used this word in a 1940 song. He told me, 'This is the word that I've brought to songs, and before me it was never used!' Literally, in Urdu, it means an idol, not sweetheart or beloved. But a beloved is like an idol that is worshipped. So in poetry, 'sanam' is used for the beloved. Another popular word for the 'beloved' is 'pia', which is a colloquial version of the Sanskrit word 'priya', which means 'dear'.

NMK: How much of a poetic style can you have in your songwriting?

JA: That depends. We must remember that a film song is not only written for a situation but also for a character. The character may be a villager or a Bombay street urchin, a cabaret dancer, or a villager. You must have command over the language so that the song's vocabulary matches the spoken language of various characters.

What is the kind of a character you are writing the song for? What is his or her intellectual level? How educated or uneducated is this hero or heroine? The question of characterization has to be taken into consideration. For example, when the director of *Lagaan*, Ashutosh Gowariker, narrated the story of the film to me, I understood the kind of cultural background the screen characters were from—and when writing the songs for the film, I used the same kind of language used in dialogue—so the songs had an Awadhi flavour.

NMK: Do you always try to write the song in a vocabulary that is close to the spoken dialogue?

JA: To a certain extent, if it is possible, but after that one should not even try. It might compromise the quality of the song.

There was a film called *Bada Din*—a story about Christians from Bengal who speak in pidgin Hindustani—'Tooti phooti hindustani'—and say things like 'Hum bolne ko sakta hai'. Now I had two choices: should I write in this style or should I write in grammatically correct but simple language? The audience would not accept this character singing a ghazal for instance. So I decided to use simple but correct language. If I had chosen the first option, the song might have been convincing in the film, but it would not have had a life beyond the film.

NMK: I found your songs in *Dil Chahta Hai* quite unexpectedly poetic for the so-called cool characters.

JA: I don't agree. 'Cool' isn't the opposite of poetic. Somehow people have come to believe that one can either be modern or literary. And that so-called cool characters will sing inane and mundane words, this isn't true at all. It's wrong to assume that

young people are insensitive to poetry. They just don't want
to go over the top. They have developed a preference for the
understatement. They don't want crudity—even crudity of
sorrow. A display of emotion embarrasses them.

NMK: What is this embarrassment?

JA: What I've noticed about this generation is that they have
seen such crude forms of melodrama written by my generation
and the previous one that they have developed an aversion to
melodrama. They are rather secretive about their emotions
and feelings. And we're so stupid that we tend to believe that
they are not emotional at all. It isn't true. They want emotions
to be expressed without melodrama or overt sentimentality.
Melodrama has gone out of fashion. But cold-blooded cynicism
and inane, meaningless, tasteless songs and screenplays must
not replace it. Melodrama should be replaced by dignified,
understated, emotional drama and smart, sensitive, and
unpretentious lyrics. That's what I feel.

NMK: What must you always bear in mind when writing
a song?

JA: That we are ultimately writing for a large audience. So if
you write a stanza in which the sense is only revealed in the last
line as in poetry, an untrained listener might get confused. In
poetry, this works. In a film song, you have to give meaning in a
more transparent and direct way.

That said, I think people are open to a very literary song, but
the words should not be abstract. They should understand what
you are talking about. If they can understand the whole song,
then they won't mind if there are a few unfamiliar words in it.
Like 'aafreen'—you'll find hundreds and thousands of people
who don't know the meaning of the word.

NMK: I didn't know it myself. When I asked you, you said it
meant 'wow'.

JA: Yes! [*both laugh*]

NMK: There is probably a more poetic translation than 'wow'.

The fact that you choose words to be sung—because a song is not a poem that will be read or dialogue that will be spoken—does that influence your diction?

JA: Some words don't sound right for particular notes. The word may in fact sound prosaic and unmusical. Many words are dry and static. So you must create a phonetic impact in a way that the words keep flowing with the tune. When writing prose, you can say, 'Paayal ki chhan-chhan' [The jingling of anklet bells], but this may not sound right in a song.

For instance, some word endings may sound abrupt—take 'b' in 'matlab' [meaning]. Any word that ends with a 'b' cuts sharply. You have to be careful about how you use these sounds and take care that harsher words are softened by a vowel. Add the word 'aaya' [came] to 'matlab' and it makes the sound of the 'b' more fluid. So now 'matlab' melts away and moves forward. Otherwise, it would stand still and have the effect of crushing bricks.

For example, a word ending with the letter 'k' can sound dry. Like 'tak' [until]. If you use a word ending with 'm'—like sanam , here the lips meet at the end of the word, and the 'm' can resound in a kind of hum. This is like a slow dissolve. The word 'sanam' is softer and blends seamlessly into the next word. It is musical.

NMK: You seem attracted by echoing words such as 'Paayaliya chhun-mun, chhun-mun'. I believe these words 'chhun-mun' do not mean anything in themselves but evoke the sound of anklets. Is that right?

JA: Echoing words are used in spoken language, and you can use them creatively. The meaning of words is important but so is their phonetic effect in a song.

I believe every sound has a certain colour and visual effect. If you take the sound of 'cha', it has a sparkle that's somewhat yellow or golden, while the sparkle of 'ja' is very white. 'Ta' sounds like throwing a ball on a solid surface, but throw that same ball on wet ground, you'll hear a 'tha' sound. If you hit the ball against a hollow surface, you'll hear a 'dha'. Sounds create different images in your mind. Overusing 'ka' within a line can make the effect dry. 'Dha' is a sticky sound, 'gha' is a dense sound, 'ga' is a clean one.

NMK: Why do you sometimes choose to repeat the same word in a line—say 'Khoya-khoya' [lost, wistful]?

JA: It is interesting to repeat a word if the musical note is recurring as well—you'll find an example in Shyam Benegal's film *Zubeidaa*. The song 'Dheeme-dheeme gaaon' [Softly, softly, I sing] composed by A.R. Rahman had this repetition. The other example is 'Ghir-ghir aayi badariya kaari' [Dark clouds have covered the sky] in *Sardari Begum*.

In fact, I have written a number of songs in which I have repeated the same word. If the notes are saying the same thing, the same word may be used twice, and it will sound all right. I only repeat words that are part of spoken language like 'hauley-hauley' [softly, softly], 'dheere-dheere' [quietly, quietly] or 'aahista-aahista' [slowly, slowly].

NMK: When we look at films, we can easily say that such and such film is dated. Can we say the same for words—do some words have a sell-by date too?

JA: That's very interesting. Words change with different generations. Some words go out of fashion and others come into vogue. That's true in literature and in film lyrics. You realize that a word has become obsolete because your sense of aesthetics and values has changed. The whole ambience and atmosphere keeps changing. At the start of the talkies, when film songs were looking for a point of reference, the thumris, the kajris, and the ghazals became that point of reference. Then fashions changed.

NMK: When we speak of the ghazal, we're of course talking about a lyric poem in Urdu. I believe the word 'ghazal' literally means 'a romantic address to the beloved'.

Can we qualify the 'thumri' as belonging to a light classical tradition, whereas the 'kajri' is traditionally a musical form originating in eastern UP and Bihar and usually associated with the rainy season, is that right?

JA: Exactly. The musical traditions of the thumri and the kajri borrowed their vocabulary or expression from folk songs because there was no other source. The ghazal had other sources. In classical singing, when words were included, their words and diction come from the folk song.

When sound came to Hindi/Urdu cinema, the musical references—the thumri, the kajri, and the ghazal—came originally from the urban Urdu-Parsee theatre. This theatrical tradition was the inspiration for the early Indian talkies, as we have discussed.

Our basic narrative structure and characters, the hero, heroine, villain, and comedian, and songs are also from that theatrical tradition. So it was natural that the early film songs depended on a similar vocabulary and expression. This carried on for a while, then other factors came into play.

NMK: What triggered the change in the vocabulary of film songs?

JA: The urbanization of the Indian cine-goer. Audiences who had urban aspirations started rejecting words that had rural roots. Take words that mean the 'beloved' like 'balma' and 'sajna'—if you trace these words, they come from a rural context and background—they are ambassadors of the Indian folk song. Gradually words that had a touch of the rural were pruned and finally removed and an increasingly urban language entered the film song.

Progressive poets like Sahir and Majrooh have played a very important role in expediting the urbanization of film lyrics. At a later stage, in the mid-1960s, the other important lyricist who brought this change and whom we have talked about was Anand Bakshi. He kept the song urban but also, to some extent, took it away from the Urdu poetry tradition. Anand Bakshi brought the song closer to conversational Hindustani as spoken in big cities. So obviously all the 'balmas' [beloveds] were left far behind. Now we have many cultural walls between 'balma' and the Hindi film song. But sometimes 'balma' still sneaks in. The word 'sajna' is still more frequently used, as it perhaps does not have a village ring phonetically, although both words mean the same thing.

NMK: Cinemas were largely in urban areas and patronized by city dwellers, so what do you mean by the 'urbanization' of the audience?

JA: It's true that at any point of time, cinema has been a city activity, and films have been patronized for the most part by the urban middle class. But the middle class in the 1930s till the 1950s was of a different composition and originated from a particular kind of milieu. This was the time of pre-industrialization, and in those days, the urban middle class was just the extended family of the landed gentry. They came from a feudal background, and their connections with a rural ethos were strong. With the abolition of the zamindari [feudal] system and the growth of industrialization, the middle classes finally severed ties with their rural cousins, and from that time, a new middle class emerged with no connections to rural India. Increased industrialization also meant that many of the working classes entered the middle-income groups. These people had neither a romantic image of village India nor did they indulge in the nostalgia associated with it.

NMK: The breaking of ties with rural India must have increased with each new generation.

JA: It did. Here, I must point out that the language of the Hindi film has always been Hindustani, leaning towards Urdu, right from the first 'talkie' *Alam Ara*. Urdu, by temperament, has always been urban, but writers and lyricists like Arzoo Lucknavi who worked for studios like New Theatres in Calcutta synthesized Urdu with rural dialects. For example, take the stanza in Pankaj Mullick's famous 'Yaad aaye ki na aaye tumhaari' [Whether I miss you or not]:

Jhadte hain phool phaagun ke
Phaagun ke maheene mein
Main tum se juda hota hoon
Ik dard liye seene mein
[Flowers wither in the autumn
In the month of Phagun
I part from you
With an aching heart]

The metaphor in the first line is rural, whilst the diction of the second line is purely urban. With the progressive Urdu poets, the balance tilted towards an urban and modern expression. For example, Ali Sardar Jafri and Majrooh Sultanpuri together wrote a song in the film *Footpath*:

Shaam-e-gham ki qasam aaj ghamgeen hain hum
Aa bhi ja aa bhi ja aaj mere sanam
[I swear by this evening of melancholy, sad am I
Come to me now, my beloved]

While Sahir's *Baazi* song went like this:

> Tadbeer se bigdi hui taqdeer bana le
> Apne pe bharosa hai to ye daao laga le
> [Transform your misfortune to good fortune
> Trust in yourself and throw the dice]

NMK: What about the influence of the ghazal on film songs?

JA: The ghazal is usually written in 12–14 different metres. Since all the lines are equal, this did not provide much variety for music directors. By the 1950s, other musical influences were seeping into Hindi film music. So we see composers like C. Ramachandra, O.P. Nayyar, and later R.D. Burman introducing Western and Latin American music. When some tunes became less Indian and more unconventional, the ghazal was inevitably marginalized. Today, if you have a ghazal in a film, people may find the tune monotonous and the expression old-fashioned. Perhaps the ghazal sounds too simple nowadays to the ears of film directors or producers.

Recent movies also do not allow much space for the ghazal. The fast pace of films is at the cost of depth and substance. In a frantic speed of narration, obviously you cannot have slow and introspective songs. After all, film music is a part of the narrative and must reflect its tempo. Songs are now sung at such great speed, with the tune moving like lightning, that the words hardly register. Only when the music is at peace with itself, when there is some time to ponder upon the words, that words take on an importance. Under those circumstances, the ghazal can find a place again in cinema. Besides, post-independence, the kind of step-motherly treatment that Urdu has received at the hands of the political establishment has considerably reduced its space.

NMK: What do you mean by this?

JA: The kind of education that has become prevalent in the last few decades and the sorts of social priorities that have emerged in the 1970s and 1980s have resulted in the fact that we have a generation unfamiliar with poetry. This is true of the audience as well as those working in films, including many producers and directors. I am afraid, they don't have the ear for language and poetry that perhaps the 1950s' and 1960' directors and composers once had.

That said, if a well-composed ghazal is heard, it is appreciated even today. People may have lost a degree of sensitivity, but poetry has not entirely lost its magic.

NMK: Coming back to your songs, I have noticed that you create a romantic mood but often do not express love directly. An intimate mood is created on screen and then your song says 'Kuchh na kaho' [Don't say a word].

JA: You can never describe an emotion. It's not possible. You may try to describe emotion, but it will have boundaries. The very fact that you are defining it places emotion in a boundary. But if you leave emotion to the imagination, then it becomes much larger.

NMK: When writing romantic songs, do you think one needs to be in love, or is knowing how to access emotions enough?

JA: You have to put yourself in that frame of mind. Intuitively, you will know that a particular word is not strong enough. Or it is harsh, or it will make the thought prosaic. The word will break the magic. You must have that kind of understanding.

I think, with time, I've developed a little more confidence. Practice has made me write to the tunes with greater ease. When I started writing songs, there were so many people who felt a certain reservation. They believed my songs would be too poetic! This was their complaint. I am pleased this flaw has

been accepted, and I'm fortunate that the people I work with
have accepted the songs the way that I wanted to write them.

NMK: You have also written songs in the question–answer
form. For instance, 'Jaane kyun log pyaar karte hain?' [I wonder
why people fall in love] for *Dil Chahta Hai*. What freshness does
this form bring to the classic love duet?

JA: Why are two people singing to each other in the first
place? I feel the song must stir the desire in the other to
respond. The question and answer form provides a reason for
the girl to respond to the boy or vice-versa. This allows you
to build and layer the song. I have written a song like this in
Lakshya—'Is baat ko agar tum zara ghuma-phira ke kehte to
achcha hota' [If you had found a roundabout way of saying this,
it would have been better].

'It's not a new technique. As you know, Sahir wrote songs in
this style—remember the superb *Pyaasa* song?

Man: Hum aap ki aankhon mein is dil ko basa den to?
Woman: Hum moond ke palkon ko is dil ko saza den to?
[Man: What if I gave my heart to you?
Woman: What if I punished your heart by discarding it?]

The lovers question each other in song as though they were
having a conversation.

And there's 'Abhi na jao chhod kar' [Don't go and go]
or the *Sasural* song by Shailendra, 'Ik sawaal main karoon,
ik sawaal tum karo' [I'll ask you a question, you ask me a
question]. This form of song has been written in the past and
gives a sense of progression.

NMK: The expression of romance has changed a lot in recent
times. The days of *Chaudhvin ka Chand* are over. There's much
more physicality depicted on the screen, much more overt
sexuality. Half a century later, what's gone out of romance?

JA: Romantic pining is diminishing. There was a time when there were so many social restrictions and obstacles, sometimes created by the family and sometimes by society, that couples had to rely on fantasies and dreams. Today the need to fantasize has decreased, but romance is not a thing of the past.

Young people still fall in love; couples still misunderstand each other and miss each other when they're apart. They feel hurt and pain. Maybe the expression has changed, but emotions such as happiness, sorrow, the desire to possess, a sense of loss, the triumph of victory, the sting of defeat in love—none of that has not gone out of fashion. It cannot. Human beings are programmed to fall in love and be romantic. And believe me, the younger generation are human beings too. [both laugh]

NMK: Clearly, film songs are important to you. But when you and Salim Khan wrote the best screenplays in the 1970s, why was there so little room for songs in your films? The dialogue is excellent, full of metaphor, pun, and dramatic turn of phrase, but what about the space for songs?

JA: That's rather interesting. I think your observation carries a lot of weight. Yes, it is a fact that in our early screenplays, there was hardly any room for songs.

There was that one famous number in *Zanjeer* sung by Manna Dey, 'Yaari hai imaan mera yaar meri zindagi' [Friendship is my religion and my friend is dear as my life], but none of our movies can boast of great music. It was not the fault of the composer or the lyricist, but there was hardly any scope within the narrative for songs because most scenes were hijacked by dialogue. [both smile]

NMK: It seems to me that Amitabh Bachchan's delivery in the famous temple scene in *Deewaar* was spoken as though he were reciting a poem in a mushaira. His intonation and pace was like an angry poet speaking. Do you agree?

JA: In the last two or three decades, there has been a new recipe that's been going around called 'prose poetry'. It is purely prose. I don't understand what the meaning of prose poetry is. It is like saying hot cold, dead alive, or black white. Perhaps a monologue is within the realm of this expression. Shall we say, a good monologue always has the possibility of sounding like prose poetry?

NMK: Then came the 1980s, which was a pretty dire time for Indian films and film music. Would you agree?

JA: The situation for the film song in the mid-1980s had deteriorated so much that even light-hearted songs started sounding like classical poetry. I'd rather not mention the names of particular films, producers, or directors, but having agreed to work on some films, I withdrew when I heard the song situations. I abhor crudity and crassness.

The 1980s were indeed a terrible period for Hindi film songs. There was a drop in aesthetic and literary values. Songs with double-meanings lyrics, bordering on obscenity, vulgarity, crossing all lines of decency, had come into fashion. I put my foot down and made it clear to everyone, 'Come what may, I will not write such songs.' Because of this, some people thought that I was being difficult and sitting on a high horse. I was finally vindicated when the film *1942, A Love Story* came along. I'm thankful to the director Vidhu Vinod Chopra who offered me the movie. He gave me a free hand and allowed me to write the way I wanted. The songs went on to become huge hits, nailing the lie that audiences only like songs with double meaning.

NMK: During that same period, in the 1980s, you wrote the song 'Ek do teen' [One, two, three] in *Tezaab*. For someone who was writing literary songs, how did you suddenly start counting numbers?

JA: This song has an interesting backstory. You see music directors sing meaningless words, just to illustrate the tune, and these are called 'dummy words'. I think this term has been coined by the Indian film industry. Dummy words are used when the composer presents the tune, and instead of singing, 'la la la la', the music director sings dummy words like 'aaja aaja' or something like that.

So Laxmikant illustrated the tune by singing, 'Ek do teen chaar paanch chhe saath' [one, two, three, four, five, six, seven]. I brought the tune home on a cassette and suddenly had an idea. A line came to me: 'Tera karoon din gin-gin ke intezaar' [I count the days till you return]. The moment I hit on this line, it provided me with the angle for the whole song, so I remained loyal to it. And then the song took the form of detailing what happens on each passing day as she waits for her lover's return.

The next day, I went back to Laxmikant and said, 'I'm thinking of keeping the numbers in the lyrics.' He almost panicked and said, 'Dekhiye, dekhiye [See here], I think we're going totally overboard. It will sound ridiculous.' I reassured him, 'Leave it to me. I'll write the song in a way that will justify the use of the numbers.'

NMK: How did your literary friends react to this song?

JA: Don't ask! On numerous occasions, I have been asked, 'You're a poet and you've written such beautiful songs, how could you write a song like "Ek do teen"?' So I tell them, 'I'll recite the whole song, then decide if it still seems a meaningless, absurd song. I'll accept your verdict and apologize.' When I recite this song, everyone is surprised, even though they must have heard it hundreds of times. They had never noticed that it has a complete structure.

In the same way, I wrote another song with one main idea running through it. That was 'Ek ladki ko dekha to aisa laga' [I saw a girl who reminded me of...], and the rest of the song answers this question.

This gives you a framework, now you talk about this girl. The whole song is built around similes. When he saw her, she reminded him of a blossoming rose, etc. You create a narrative in the mukhda, and the antaras develop the story. One thought is running through the song and should be treated as one statement.

NMK: Fascinating.

It seems to me that songs no longer carry the main interest of the film.

JA: Yes, the song is gradually ceasing to contribute to the story. When a hero and heroine meet, you cut to some fantasy and imaginary world: they're dancing and singing, and then you cut back to the action. You are not adding to their relationship through song. Maybe you have shown a great moment of spectacle, but the song has become largely a sideshow and not part of the narrative.

I'm not a person who is afraid of outside influences—I mean Western influences. Nor do I believe that MTV or Channel V will destroy us. Nonsense! Nothing of the sort will happen. But we had developed a unique style of picturizing songs. It was unbelievably good. Directors like Guru Dutt, Vijay Anand, and Raj Khosla had a superb way of picturizing songs. And I am genuinely very disappointed and upset to see that we are not carrying forward that tradition. In Indian theatre, songs were part of the drama and were given the same weight as a scene. So Indian cinema furthered this tradition by using music within the drama. Now we're aping music videos and the songs in today's films cease to have a real function within the story. The song has become a kind of a perk that's offered with the film.

NMK: Why is this happening?

JA: We live in an era of throwaway lighters, and we use them and forget them. That's the fate of most things, including music. And that's why much of the appeal of recent music does not last for a long time, because it has no staying power. It comes [*clicks his fingers*], it entertains you—it rarely entertains me—then it vanishes. It doesn't enter your psyche because it has no time to do so. The tempo is too fast for that. If the tune does not give enough space to the words, if the tune does not allow you to reflect, 'Oh my God, this is what the song is saying', it won't stay with you for long. You may tap your feet to the tune, and then you'll forget it. I'm not saying the tunes should be as slow as Saigal's songs—but you could strike a balance.

NMK: Tell me, what is good about the recent songs that did not exist previously?

JA: The technical standard of recording, the orchestration, the reproduction of music is much better. There's no doubt about it. But I am afraid the same cannot be said about the lyrics—the music has become a little too frenetic. I don't like it. I think we should have more confidence. We may need some songs with a fast tempo—if the scene requires it—but why must every song be so frantic? Perhaps the lack of good stories with a genuine emotional content demand this frenzy. The stories themselves do not offer enough situations in which songs can have emotional depth. The stories are hurried and have no room for contemplative songs. Most films are desperate to entertain, so the 'item' song has taken on great importance. I feel a good song is like good wine. The effect must be unhurried.

Quality songs like the ones in *Pyaasa* were only possible in *Pyaasa* and in no other kind of film. However, if you listen to a totally mediocre song of the 1950s, even that has a certain finesse of language, while today that quality is missing.

Thankfully, we have rejected vulgar and crude songs. And I think from the time of the 1980s, things have moved somewhat in the right direction, but there is still much room for improvement.

NMK: What are the forces behind this change—is it because of market forces, the audience, or the music companies?

JA: You cannot blame any one factor. Nevertheless, I must say that some music companies, if not all, are responsible, by and large, for what's happening. It is contrary to the rules of the market, but there was a time when only HMV had the monopoly over film music in India. But there was no interference from them. Now they are around six major music companies. Logic dictates that since there's no longer a monopoly, there should be less control. But the reality is quite the opposite. Today the big bosses of music companies quite often have the final say on the tune and words and not the director. It's shocking.

NMK: Would you say this been your experience?

JA: Yes. A particular 'company-wallah', whom I do not wish to name, once came to a music session and started suggesting certain words for the song to me. I told him, 'I have a very dear friend, Mr Naresh Goyal, who owns a commercial airline called Jet Airways. It is the fastest-growing passenger airline in the world, but I have never seen Naresh Goyal entering the cockpit and instructing a pilot about how he should fly. He hires professional pilots and trusts them. So Mr Moneybags, you may be the owner of a music company, you may know how to sell CDs, but that makes you a salesman, not a musician or a poet.'

NMK: How did he react?

JA: He didn't like it, of course! But I had to react because I genuinely believe that marketing people should not try to dictate the creative process—it is not healthy.

NMK: Is there a link between commercial pressures and the fact that most of the songs today are dance numbers?

JA: It's the obsession for speed. Whether it's the screenplay or the performance, everything must be fast. People think that any stillness in the song will lose the viewer's attention. You must have noticed how fast the song is cut nowadays? Plus there are so many wide shots that you are left guessing which star is performing the song on the screen. In my childhood, I remember coming home from school and sometimes hearing street hawkers crying out at top speed, selling their wares. They were selling kohl, toothpaste, or hair lotion, and they never stopped chatting for a second. They believed that the minute they paused for breath, the crowd gathered around them would disappear. We have become like those street hawkers.

NMK: The use of 'double meaning' in Hindi film lyrics has really caught on. But must the lines always suggest something vulgar and often sexist? There are fabulously intelligent examples of the use of 'double meaning' in some English lyrics. I'm thinking of a John Lennon line, 'She's not a girl who misses much'. This line can either mean that nothing escapes her or that she is so self-contained that she never allows herself to be emotionally attached to anything or anyone.

JA: This term 'double meaning' has also developed a double meaning in Hindi film songs. One layer of meaning points to a harmless, innocuous statement, and the other is profane, vulgar, and often obscene. That is what double meaning has come to denote in most Hindi film songs. In poetry, traditionally there is the use of 'zu-maanviyat', which literally means double meaning or double entendre. All the great masters of poetry like Ghalib have written so many couplets, poems, and ghazals that are wide open to various interpretations. People are still writing about Ghalib's poetry and finding new meanings in his work. There are different schools of thought about what Ghalib had intended in this or that couplet. Let's look at one example:

Hum kahan ke daana the, kis hunar mein yakta the
Be-sabab hua Ghalib dushman aasman apna.

It is an accepted interpretation that 'aasman' [sky], the symbol of destiny, can be quite often unkind. Now let us see Ghalib's couplet in that light. Ghalib says, 'I am not a genius or master of any art, why should destiny choose to turn against me?' On one level, it is an expression of great humility, while, in fact, he is suggesting that he is indeed a genius and master of art. Ghalib wants the reader to protest, 'Of course, Ghalib, you are a genius!'

I find it amusing that some people write songs either with double meaning or no meaning at all. For the moment, let's put aside our disdain and look at these so-called double-meaning songs. In fact, such songs belong to an old tradition and were not invented by film people. In Indian folk music, we have dozens of examples. In the old days, during a marriage ceremony, people would abuse one another in songs. These were extremely vulgar songs about the future in-laws, the groom, and the bride and her family. People would laugh wholeheartedly at their implicit vulgarity. But these songs were limited to intimate surroundings and did not enter the mainstream. Such songs were not heard on the radio or seen on television. They were not in films either.

NMK: If such songs have always been sung, what difference does it make if they are in the movies?

JA: What worries me is that—all right—someone wrote the song 'Choli ke peechhe kya hai?' [What's behind your blouse?] in the film Khalnayak, and someone else composed the music. A playback singer sang the song and it appeared in the film performed by an actress. Now if you count all the people involved, there cannot be more than a dozen. In a million people, if there were a dozen people who have a penchant for vulgar songs, it would not bother me or anyone else. But the alarming thing was that the song became a huge hit. Millions and millions of people across society made it a super hit and that bothers me. Similar songs have been sung for centuries, but the whole of society did not lap them up.

NMK: What does this tell us about the way society is developing?

JA: I believe that at any point in history, we can see that art, literature, and music and the contemporary socio-political movements are not in watertight compartments. They reflect one another. There was a sort of moral decline in the 1980s. Our sense of values had nose-dived. There is no doubt that in those years, the worst kind of film was being made in India, and by and large, the worst kind of film music was appreciated. Compare this era to the 1950s, a time when the best film songs were written. A time when culture, decency, and idealism prevailed, those were the days of Jawaharlal Nehru.

NMK: What about the now established generation of directors—the ones you have worked with—are they able to raise the level and understand the nuances of language, understand metaphors and symbols?

JA: Take the successful directors like Karan Johar, Nikhil Advani, Farah Khan, Farhan Akhtar, and Ashutosh Gowariker. I can see that their individual understanding of language differs. But they have a refined sense of aesthetics, although many times when they are confronted with a word that is completely alien to their own vocabulary, they are slightly taken aback. Sometimes they are reluctant to use it in the song. But I'm relieved that somehow they've developed some confidence in me. They trust my judgement and I'm grateful for that. But I wonder what they'd do with a writer in whom they do not have the same kind of trust.

NMK: What would you say is your overriding contribution to Hindi films songs?

JA: It's difficult and awkward for me to compliment my own work. That would not be right, no matter how objective I try to be. But in all humility, I can say that I have tried to encourage a certain level of decency, a sense of aesthetic values, and when possible, maintain a certain literary flavour in my songs. At the risk of sounding immodest—I would say that I have not written any vulgar or obscene lines. Over the years, I think I have developed a better command over the medium and so my craft has improved. I can understand the most complicated tune and know how to divide it and write a song on it. I did not know how to do this before, and this was a great challenge for me. Once the intricacy and complexity of the tune were no longer intimidating, I became more at ease. So I suppose that relaxed quality—that ease—must be coming through my work. But I am mindful that this ease should not result in complacency. So I keep listening to the old songs of the masters of the 1950s and 1960s. They remind me how much more there is to be done.

NMK: Have songs come to you in a dream?

JA: I don't remember such productive dreams. [both laugh] But one thing that has definitely happened to me—I have listened to a tune two or three times and have taken a break, slept for an hour, got up, and then written the song. You internalize the tune, you know the song's context in the movie, and when you sleep for a while, the subconscious works.

NMK: If you were stranded on a desert island with one record, what would it be?

JA: One thing is for sure, it would be an LP! [both laugh]

NMK: Brilliant idea!

You have written so many songs, is there a landmark song?

JA: This is not just a diplomatic answer. But as a matter of fact, every song is a challenge and I try to do my best in every song. How far I succeed is for others to decide. But the songs that have been highly appreciated are: 'Ek ladki ko dekha to aisa laga' or 'Ghar se nikalte hi', and 'Sandese aate hain' [Messages come].

'Kuchh na kaho' [Don't say a word] is one of my favourite songs. The songs in Sardari Begum were a totally different experience for me. When Shyam Benegal said he wanted me to write the lyrics for his film, I happily accepted, but I didn't tell him how frightened I was. I had to write thumris, kajris, and horis, which had to sound as though they were traditional songs. I was also asked to write a ghazal because Sardari Begum sings a ghazal in the film. We had nine songs in the film. And believe me, Munni, in the morning I used to go to the recording theatre without a written word, without an inkling of what I was going to do. The music director would sit; the singers and the musicians and we would develop the song right then and there. In five days, we recorded nine songs.

NMK: It must have been a fulfilling experience.

Your father, Jaan Nisar Akhtar, passed away in 1976, some four years before you started writing film songs. Do you find any similarity between his style of songwriting and yours?

JA: Yes, but not always. Sometimes I write certain lines that I think are close to his writing style. In the song from Saagar, 'Saagar jaisi aankhon waali' [The girl with eyes as deep as the ocean], there is a line, 'tere sapne dekh raha hoon, aur mera ab kaam hai kya?' [I am lost in dreams of you, what other purpose could I have?]

I think the structure and thought of this line is very close to his style. His idea of romance was surrender. I am convinced that romance is equally possible without surrender. There have been times when I have used an expression that perhaps my father would have used.

He wrote some excellent songs including the *Razia Sultan* song, 'Ae dil-e-naadaan' [O innocent heart], 'Ye dil aur unki nigaahon ke saaye' [My heart is under the shadow of her gaze] from *Prem Parbat*, and 'Aankhon hi aankhon mein ishaara ho gaya' [An exchange of glances has said it all] from *C.I.D.*

NMK: So you inherited poetry from your father.

JA: And he inherited it from his father! As I mentioned, Muztar Khairabadi, my grandfather, was considered a master in his time and was an extraordinary poet. He could create couplet after couplet extempore with no effort at all. He once wrote a ghazal that had perhaps the longest metre in the world. A single line of that ghazal filled an entire page. It was made up of eight couplets. He wrote romantic ghazals as well as poetry in praise of Allah. He wrote a complete book of verse in praise of the Holy Prophet and, at the same time, he wrote many songs in celebration of Lord Krishna. You might remember my grandfather was a Sessions Judge, so sometimes he would give legal verdicts entirely in verse. They have preserved one of his verdicts in verse at the museum of Tonk, which was a princely state in Rajasthan.

NMK: I can see where you inherited your ease in writing songs like 'Breathless'.

By the way, did your grandfather ever write for films?

JA: No, he died in 1927—four years before India's first 'talkie'. But my grandfather's poetry was used in the film *Deedar*. Shakeel Badayuni wrote the songs and the music was composed by Naushad. In the film, there was a famous song by Mohammed Rafi, performed on the screen by Dilip Kumar. 'Hue hum jin ke liye barbaad' [My life has been ruined for her sake]. In those days there was a tradition to start a song with a doha [couplet]. This doha would not necessarily be written by the lyricist who wrote the rest of the song. So the doha in 'Hue hum jin ke liye barbaad' was written by my grandfather and begins like this:

Aseer-e-panjaye ahed-e shabab kar ke mujhe
Kahaan gaya mera bachpan kharaab kar ke mujhe
[Imprisoning me in the claws of intoxicating youth
Having undone my life, where has my childhood flown?]

There is a ghazal popularly known as written by Bahadur Shah Zafar, but anyone familiar with the history of Urdu literature knows that this ghazal 'Na kisi ki aankh ka noor hoon, na kisi ke dil ka qaraar hoon' [I am not the light in the eyes of someone, nor am I the solace of another's heart] was written by my grandfather. Many people, including one of the most respected authorities of Urdu, Aal Ahmed Suroor has said in one of his articles that this ghazal has been erroneously credited to Bahadur Shah Zafar.

NMK: We talked about your growing up years and how poetry was so much a part of it. Did you happen to meet any of the great poets of earlier times?

JA: As a child, I heard Josh reciting his poetry, and Jigar too. I heard Firaq and Makhdoom recite poetry. As I mentioned to you, I was fortunate to know Sahir, Ali Sardar Jafri, Kaifi, and Majrooh very well, and of course I knew my maternal uncle, Majaz.

I had memorized hundreds of couplets by heart and could recite them by the time I was twelve.

NMK: Clearly you were totally immersed in poetry. For someone who is unfamiliar with poetry, how would you explain the difference between poetry and prose?

JA: This can be answered in two ways: a poetic and a prosaic manner!

What makes poetry different to prose is that it has a certain discipline. It has a certain rhyme and inherent music. There was a time when poetry was constrained in certain metres. Those rules are broken. Although what is called blank verse, or free verse, may have got rid of traditional metres, it is not free of poetry. The difference between poetry that sticks to a metre and free verse is the difference between a geet [song], which has equal lines, and a raag that a classical singer sings. In a raag, the taans [melodic patterns] are not of the same length, but their scanning is the same. A taan, whether long or short, will end on a particular beat—what we call 'sum' [the first beat of a rhythmic cycle]. In free verse or blank verse, the inherent music, the beat, will remain. Free verse, just as in classical singing, has no rhyme, but it cannot do away with rhythm.

For me poetry is like the dream of language. What is a dream? When one sleeps, all the parts of the body continue to function: the heart, the stomach, the liver. If the brain stops functioning, we would die. So the brain keeps working, but then how will you sleep? So nature has found a strange way. When you sleep, your mind starts talking to you in a different language and that language is the dream. In the same way, poetry has that dream-like quality. It gives solace, peace, and pleasure, and at the same time, it makes one reflect.

Like dreams, poetry talks in symbols. It gives hints. It enters the subconscious mind and connects to a world layered with memories and emotional experiences. Between countries there is a no-man's-land, and I think the same space exists between the conscious and the subconscious mind. Poetry grows there. And if those who listen to, or who read poetry are receptive, it reaches the no-man's-land in their minds. There are some conscious reasons why a poem is appreciated, but there are certain reasons that are not so obvious. And you say quite helplessly, 'Is mein kuchh ajeeb baat hai'—there is some strange charm to it. That charm is because the poem has appealed to the subconscious mind and stirred dormant feelings, thoughts, and memories.

In poetry, each word can trigger an association in the subconscious and in the realm of feelings. Good writers and poets instinctively know what kind of allusions words can evoke. There must also be a balance of sounds. For instance, some light words like 'ehsaas' [to feel] and 'mehsoos' [to sense] do not have strong consonants. So the lightest breeze can blow the line away. In order to keep the words grounded, light words need strong consonants. They work like paperweights.

NMK: When you began writing poetry, did you look to the classics of Urdu poetry and regard yourself as part of that tradition or did you regard yourself as belonging to the contemporary world?

JA: I have read traditional Urdu poetry and poetry written by the poets of the Progressive Writers' Movement. I have also read modern and postmodern poetry. When the Progressive Writers' Movement started, the traditionalists rejected it. When modern poetry came into existence around the 1960s, poets who were rebels themselves once upon a time looked down on this kind of poetry. I am influenced by all three groups and can see some truth and some validity in each one.

As far as the traditional poets are concerned, the kind of symbols, the kind of language and craft they developed is mind-blowing. Poets like Ghalib and Mir had tremendous socio-political consciousness, as we have discussed. But when poetry dealt more directly with social issues, the puritan, the traditionalist, found it slightly too prosaic. On the other hand, the progressive poets believed if art did not have a socio-political consciousness, then it was reactionary. At the 22nd Congress in Moscow, Khrushchev spoke against Stalin and about the process of de-Stalinization. It showed that god had feet of clay. Then the conflict between India and China in the 1960s shook the foundations of the leftist movements in India to a great extent. There were many other factors; perhaps the writers themselves were getting disillusioned. The Red Revolution they had believed would follow independence never happened. And the contradictions of the Communist movement were becoming obvious in the international arena.

So, broadly, I would say my influences have been traditional poetry, the work of the Progressive Writers' Movement, and the poets who came after that. You are a plagiarist if one poet influences you, but if a hundred poets or a movement of poetry influences you, you are a great researcher and scholar. [*both laugh*]

NMK: What do you think of the way Hindi cinema depicts Urdu poets?

JA: I am tired of it. The Urdu poets are usually drunks living in some kind of a make-believe world, and if they love, they're in love with a prostitute. This is not an Urdu poet.

If you look at contemporary Indian literature, Urdu is perhaps the most progressive language of the subcontinent. Almost all known Urdu poets were secular liberals and leftists. The Progressive Writers' Movement was not an Urdu Writers' Movement—it was an all-India movement.

We have talked about the Urdu literature that was produced during the freedom movement—all those songs/poems like

'Saare jahaan se achha hindustan humaara' [Our India is better than any other place in the world] written by the Urdu poet Iqbal. If you take the Urdu ghazal, it is often agnostic if not atheistic. The basic concern of the Urdu poet in the last 70–90 years has not been the mehbooba [the beloved] and mehboob ki galiyaan [the lane where the beloved lives] but socio-political issues.

NMK: Do you think Urdu poetry is still popular?

JA: Absolutely. Someone has done some research and discovered that of all the poetry quoted in the Lok Sabha in the past 50 years, 97 per cent is Urdu poetry.

NMK: Do you remember Ismail Merchant's film *In Custody*? The film is very much about the decline of the Urdu literary tradition. Why did that happen?

JA: Europe is predominantly Christian, but it's made up of different nations. For some illogical reason, it was decided in India during the last hundred years that religion is the basis for nations. Extreme right-wingers—both Hindu and Muslim—propagated this theory. We'll cut the story short, because it is a saga in itself—but this kind of thinking culminated in the Partition of India on religious grounds. Since they had decided that Hindus and Muslims are two different nations, they had to deny any shared culture or heritage. There was a deliberate attempt to create a false separation between their common histories and cultures. The extreme-right Hindus called Urdu 'Muslim' and the extreme-right Muslims also called it 'Muslim'.

In 1798, Shah Abdul Qadir of Delhi translated the Quran for the first time into Urdu. This was seven hundred years *after* the Quran had been translated into Sindhi. The Ulema, the religious scholars, of the time gave the Urdu translator a fatwa for translating the Quran into what was seen as a heretic language.

NMK: A heretic language?

JA: That is how fundamentalists react no matter what caste or community they belong to. A hundred and fifty years before this incident, did you know that Brahmin priests had ex-communicated Tulsidas for translating the Ramayan from Sanskrit to Awadhi, which was the language of the people?

NMK: So you think Urdu is perceived now as being synonymous with a Muslim identity?

JA: This secular language has found itself sacrificed at the altar of the two-nation theory, even though Urdu is the living proof of a truly composite culture. For the first time in the history of mankind, a language has developed a religion. But languages don't have religions—languages have regions! And Urdu became the language of a region comprising Bengal, the North West Frontier, and Sind—places with which it had no connection originally. I would not add Punjab to the list because Urdu had a strong presence there.

Eventually in Delhi, UP, and Bihar, Urdu became an alien language. It's tragic. So this was decided by politicians and by the communal politics that were prevalent at that time and, to a certain extent, are still prevalent. When I travel to Delhi or Lucknow, people say, 'Pakistani TV serials use such good language!' They're using *our* language—the language of Delhi and UP.

But Urdu is a resilient language because it is the language of the people. You cannot curb people, and despite all the bias and the prejudice against Urdu, it has survived. However, this language is not taught in many schools anymore because teachers aren't available and there is no economic advantage in knowing Urdu. And languages, I'm afraid, do not live on their literature but on their economic utility.

The baby was thrown out with the bathwater. In the last one hundred and fifty or two hundred years, north Indian urban society had developed a certain 'tehzeeb' or culture linked with Urdu—irrespective of community. When you throw out the language, the culture goes with it and a void is created, which has not been filled by anything else.

NMK: Your collection of poems *Tarkash* [Quiver] has done extremely well. In less than two years, seven editions in Hindi and three in Urdu have been published. I also believe over 100,000 copies of the audio book have sold. What more do you want in terms of a positive reaction to Urdu in India? [*JA smiles*]

JA: Well, I'm an insignificant drop in the ocean of Urdu, but I must admit that people have been kind to me and to my poetry. I started writing poetry at an age when people generally had stopped writing poetry. So it was not some passing fancy or whim. I suppose when people start writing poetry, their first phase is romantic poetry; that did not happen in my case. I was no longer at that kind of age, nor did I have that inclination. But I realize that my early poetry had a lot of nostalgia, many childhood memories, and mourning over the loss of innocence. Some friends suggested to me, 'You write well and effectively, so why not write on more important topics?' I asked them, 'Like what?' 'Social injustice, world peace, nuclear disarmament.'

There is a highly respected poet who, in a tongue-in cheek manner, called my poetry 'Mummy-Daddy ki poetry'. But I promised myself one thing, I may write good poetry or bad poetry, but I'll write what I really feel. After that period, I got over my sense of nostalgia and I wrote some poems about social injustice and the sectarian violence that's so rampant in our society. These poems were written after the Bombay riots in December and January 1991–2. The riots really stirred something in me.

NMK: I can imagine how disturbed you must have been.

JA: I think my poems reflected my shock.

NMK: I am interested that you mentioned nostalgia: do you think there is a different understanding of nostalgia that operates in writing?

JA: The ultimate thing that is said about nostalgia is that it isn't what it used to be! Most poetry or art contains a sense of loss, and if you do not experience a sense of loss, then why the need to compensate? Psychiatry believes that if you are psychologically well adjusted, you will be a good neighbour, a fine husband, a perfect father, a good friend, but not necessarily a creative person. You have to be slightly mad to fantasize and create—often you are filling a void within you.

By and large, creative people are not well adjusted to their environment and that's why I think intuitively they have a sense of nostalgia—they romanticize days that are to come and days gone by. In fact, these are merely days that do not have the power to hurt you, so you can mould them, turn them into fantasy, and make them whatever you want them to be. In poetry, you always have a wonderful future and a wonderful past. If you have a wonderful present, perhaps you would not write poetry.

NMK: Do you think creativity is a natural gift or can it be developed?

JA: I can't decide how much is inborn or how much can be nurtured. Obviously, there is something called talent, whether in singing or acting or painting. In all arts, there is an element of natural talent. But how does a person have talent? Perhaps someday, the people who are decoding genes will tell us. Obviously, talent is the essential requirement, but talent alone is not enough, training is also required. The right atmosphere provides proper training. In India, even in poetry, there was the tradition of the ustaad-shaagird. The student would write a poem and show it to the ustaad, who would point out the mistakes and change a line or two. I believe those institutions of guru-shishya are fast disappearing. We have music colleges and dance schools—everything is streamlined. But there are no schools for training poets in the way that dancing or acting classes exist.

If you have basic talent, you have to be exposed to many things. In the absence of such institutions, my advice to any young person who wants to become a poet or lyricist is that he or she must read as much poetry as possible. You must understand it and learn to appreciate it. You have to evolve a taste to appreciate the finer things. A poetry student must read classical poetry, the work of the Progressive Writers' Movement, modern and postmodern poetry. Poetry must be learned and memorized by heart. There should be hours and hours of poetry in the mind. While you read the works of many different schools, eras, and even temperaments, a vocabulary that is required will develop. Understanding the nuances of styles and of diction need to be perfected. To be a competent lyricist, these skills are required.

But all forms of creativity are an exercise in schizophrenia, because you need more than one person within you to be creative. Art needs forgetfulness, passion, involvement, and surrender. And yet it entails ability and craft that requires tremendous alertness, logic, and sharpness. You may lose yourself in creating, but a part of you is watching objectively, giving the creation proper form, editing it, pushing you in the right direction or telling you, 'No, this won't convey the right mood or feeling, this word is better.'

Say an actor is playing Hamlet on the London stage. Obviously, he has to believe that he is the Prince of Denmark. This actor has to forget that he lives somewhere off Baker Street or wherever; he has to believe he's a prince. While

Hamlet may be aware that he has an indecisive state of mind, the actor playing the role is required not to forget his chalk mark or his cue. How do you do that? One part of the actor's mind is thinking of the chalk marks, reacting to the right dialogue, and taking the five steps planned by the director, and the other part of his mind believes that he's the tormented Hamlet. You have perfect discipline and yet need to be totally lost. It's essentially paradoxical, contradictory.

The writing process cannot be demonstrated in quite the same way, because it is not a physical act. But the technique is similar. When a writer writes a song of pining, he or she identifies with the forlorn lover, but at the same time, another part of the mind is watching from a distance and guiding the process, 'Listen, don't go that way, that's a dead end. Come this side to express greater emotion.' All this happens simultaneously.

NMK: In your view are creative people aware of the process?

JA: Yes and no. Ask creative people to analyse their process of working and they would prefer not to. Perhaps all you will get is some vague answer. In some corner of the mind, an artist may know precisely how he works, but he should not think too much about it or it will spoil things. It might also be a little embarrassing to admit there was some cleverness involved in his craft. If one identifies that cleverness on a conscious level, it may help to become even smarter, but there is a danger that cold-bloodedness may creep into the creativity. Because once you understand the process of how you create something, the mystique may go away even from your own self.

NMK: How much of the personality of the writer, do you think, is discernible in his or her work?

JA: No matter how much you try to immerse yourself in the character you're writing for, your own sensibility is inevitably present in the work.

I often recite poetry in public, and after the poetry reading, there usually follows a question and answer session. I have realized that sometimes the questions are far more telling of the person who is asking than their need for answers. Every question is a statement in itself. And all questions are loaded, whether they concern literature, films, politics, or society. They reveal the biases, fears, concerns, or hopes and fantasies of the person who does the questioning.

NMK: If you had scripted this conversation, what question would you end with?

JA: [*thinks for a long while*] My last question would be: 'Where do you intend to go from here?'

It's a continuing process, one develops and changes, and whatever we've discussed is already in the past. If I live long, what will I do? I don't know whether I'll continue songwriting or start working on something else. Who knows? Energy is the thing that concerns me, and if I have the energy, I'll be able to do things. All right, I am writing songs that are appreciated. I've written some films that are remembered, but there's a lot more to do. I joined the film industry to become a director. Will I ever direct a film? I could get the backing of a producer quite easily if I wanted. But it's the fear of getting involved in something knowing it will need a lot of energy.

I suppose the answer to this last question of what next would be that some day I would like to direct a film. And if I make a good film, it will give me satisfaction, because that's what brought me to films in the first place: the desire to direct.

NMK: You would go full circle.

JA: I would like to complete the circle.

Shabana Azmi on *Talking Songs*[1]

'How can the modern and the traditional reside so comfortably in the same person? The songs of *Dil Chahta Hai* are trendy, youthful, and urban, whereas the songs in *Lagaan* are earthy, folksy, and rural. Who can believe that the two songs have been written by the same person?' exclaimed my mother[1] as she was channel-surfing one lazy afternoon at home. 'Javed has such an amazing command over the language because he is at once the city person and the small-town boy,' she stated, summarizing him adeptly.

I looked up from my cup of tea at the array of trophies lined up haphazardly on the top shelf of the bookcase in Javed's study—13 *Filmfare* awards, five National Awards, and countless others. Yet fame and recognition rest lightly on his shoulders. As I watch him, bent over his papers, penning yet another song, I realize that for somebody who has achieved so much, Javed does not hold himself precious at all.

He doesn't even have a proper desk (a temporary roll-on food table that I had once bought when my father was hospitalized still serves as his desk). He is not fussy about the

---

[1] This introduction by Shabana Azmi was the preface to *Talking Songs* published in 2002.

pen that he uses—an ordinary ballpoint or even a pencil stub suffices. The only thing he insists upon is a particular kind of unlined cheap foolscap double sheet to write on. I have often tried, without success, to replace it with simple bond paper. But he will not change it. Neither will he use one of the several hundred fountain pens that he has been gifted. When I suggest he does, he shrugs it off with 'What's the point? I will lose it and then feel miserable!'

How different he is from my father![2] Kaifi Azmi would only write at his desk—a deep mahogany writing table—and would only use a Mont Blanc pen with blue-black ink. One thing, however, that Javed has in common with my father is the family's complete access to him while he writes. All my life, I have barged into Abba's[3] room, oblivious to the demands of creativity and asked him for trivial things without ever being reprimanded. With Javed, I have become even bolder. I can interrupt him during the smallest break he takes from work to solicit his help in extricating me from a problem, whether it has to do with slum dwellers or a paragraph I am finding hard to complete. The only time he protests is when I attempt to tidy his room. His papers lie scattered all over his study—under the table, on the sofas, between hundreds of cassettes. Every time I try to bring some order into this chaos, he thunders, 'Have mercy, Shabana! Leave my papers alone. You have the whole house to clean to your heart's content, why can't you let this little room stay the way I want it?' Chastened temporarily, I leave hastily, only to sneak right back in when he is not at home to open the windows and allow some fresh air in.

Typical wife. But an atypical partner, I think. Though I might take Javed for granted as a husband, I continue to be overwhelmed by his work as a writer, poet, and lyricist. The thing that strikes me most about him is his ability to communicate the most complex of ideas in the simplest words. This has stood him in great stead as a Hindi film lyricist. He can be philosophical without being pedantic, breezy without being trivial, sensitive without being sentimental. Words come easily to him. He can write a song travelling in his car on the way to the recording studio. He can sneak away into his study in the middle of a party and emerge from his room with a freshly written song even before people have noticed his absence. I often remarked that if people knew how seemingly little effort he put into writing a song, they would never pay him! And yet, he never takes his work for granted. When faced with a challenge, he sweats through the night and is up before the sun rises.

During the shooting of *Swades*, Ashutosh Gowariker presented him with A.R. Rahman's tune at six in the evening and asked for a Ram Leela[4] song to be recorded the next morning. And this was in a hotel room in Mahabaleshwar where there were no books for reference, no time for research. Javed could only draw from his own reserves—some Ram Leelas watched in Lucknow in his childhood, some folk songs remembered from the distant past. The tension was so great to write the song that he promptly went off to sleep! Before the first rays of dawn could light up the sky, he was at work like a man possessed. The result is the remarkable.

Pal pal hai bhaari vo bipta hai aayee
[Every moment weighs heavily, we are beset with a calamity]

Like his father Jaan Nisar Akhtar, Javed can write bhajans[5] in chaste Hindi and ghazals[6] in pure Urdu, but the language he chooses to use is simple Hindustani. He is never eager to show off his mastery over vocabulary. However, he does employ with great skill, the turn and twist of phrase that only someone with a masterful command of the language can afford to do.

Raat aayee to vo jin ke ghar the
Vo ghar ko gaye so gaye
Raat aayee to ham jaise awaara phir nikle
Raahon men aur kho gaye
Is gali, us gali
Is nagar, us nagar
Jayen bhi to kahan jaana chahen agar
[Night fell, and all those who had homes
went home to sleep
Night fell, and vagabonds like us
Lost ourselves on the streets
In this lane, that lane
In this town, that town
Where would we go even if we wished to go somewhere]
(*Tezaab*)

These lines tear at my heart because I know where they come from. Countless nights spent on the streets in a hostile city; torrential rain and no roof to hide under, despite the knowledge that his father lived in the same city. 'Things without remedy should also be without regard,' he tells himself—but the dull ache in his heart refuses to go away. Years later, it surfaces and finds expression in this song from *Tezaab*. Javed's life, his struggle for survival, seems straight out of a Charles Dickens novel. There were days he had to go without food. He would land up at a friend's house and refuse to have anything to eat, opting to have a glass of water instead because he did not want to let on that he was hungry, and did not want to invite pity.

His early years were really bleak. He could have turned bitter, cynical, and hard-hearted. To his credit, he did not. He used his pain instead to creative advantage. The sorrow and hurt in Javed's work is deeply felt but always understated. And that is why it is so effective.

Hum na samjhe the baat itni si
Khwaab shishe ke duniya patthar ki
[We did not understand this simple thing
Dreams of glass, world of stone]
(Gardish)

Such economy of expression, such restraint can only come from someone who has been through the grind; someone who uses irony as a shield to protect himself from hurt. It is a recurring motif in his work and sums up the essence of Javed Akhtar.

Javed is capable of laying bare his soul without sacrificing his dignity. Like a fine sculptor he chisels his melancholy and shapes it into wistfulness.

Sach hai ke dil to dukha hai
Ham ne magar socha hai
Dil ko hai ghum kyun
Ankh hai num kyun
Hona hi tha jo hua hai
[It's true the heart has been hurt
But I wondered
Why is the heart sad?
Why is the eye moist?
What was meant to happen has happened]
(Kal Ho Na Ho)

It is this choice he makes as a writer/lyricist that sets him apart from many others today and, I think, this is one of the main reasons for his popularity. Javed is also highly regarded as a romantic writer. This is in spite of himself. Left on his own, he would use, at the most, two similes to describe his beloved. The song situation demands that he does so in 21 similes. What emerges is:

Ek ladki ko dekha to aisa laga...
[I saw a girl who reminded me of ...]
(*1942, A Love Story*)

The reason he is able to rise to the occasion with such ease is because the romantic expression is buried in his inner being. He does not allow it to surface for fear of being called sentimental. The Hindi film song gives him a release—it enables him to use, without embarrassment, poetic flourish, as in:

Dekha ek khwaab to ye silsile hue...
[I saw a dream that brought us close...]
(*Silsila*)

His romantic songs are much celebrated, but the real Javed can be discovered through the understated:

Tum ko dekha to ye khayal aaya
Zindagi dhup tum ghana saaya
[When I saw you, this thought crossed my mind
Life is the strong sun and you are the cool shade]
(*Saath Saath*)

The lines are shorn of all adornment—so simply written that they could almost pass off as dialogue—and yet every word resonates with poetry. It remains a favourite of mine.

Nasreen Munni Kabir, with her television series, *Movie Mahal*, made for Channel 4 TV in the UK, was amongst the first few who brought the magic of the Hindi film lyric into the homes in the West. Who could be more appropriate than her to speak to Javed about his work as a lyricist, and in the same spirit of her earlier book with him, *Talking Films*? She set about the task with the speed of lightning. The conversation began in Delhi, carried on in Mumbai, and was completed in London. I hope that this book will carry Javed's work to all the corners of the world where Hindi cinema is becoming a force to reckon with.

The significance of the Hindi film song and its contribution to the popularity of Hindi cinema is impossible to ignore. Javed's simple yet deeply meaningful verse has added depth and vitality to Hindi cinema. It continues to move, mesmerize, and delight.

Over the years, I have been the messenger for countless admirers who wanted me to convey to Javed how much regard they have for his work as a film lyricist. This book is for them primarily. He hardly ever talks about his work, but when he does, it is with such astounding clarity that I listen in rapt attention and learn something new each time that I hear him. And that is why this book is also for me.

Shabana Azmi

References

1. Noted stage actress Shaukat Kaifi.
2. The celebrated lyricist Kaifi Azmi.
3. 'Abba' is the Urdu for father.
4. Enactment of episode from Ramayana.
5. Hindi devotional songs.
6. Urdu love poems.

About the Authors

Javed Akhtar started his career as a screenplay writer along with his partner Salim Khan in 1971 with Ramesh Sippy's *Andaz*. Within a few years, the writing duo, Salim-Javed, had become an important force in Hindi films and had to their credit many iconic films, including *Zanjeer*, *Sholay*, *Deewaar*, and *Don*.

In 1983, the duo split up, and Javed Akhtar went on to write films on his own such as *Dacait*, *Mashaal*, *Mr India*, and *Saagar*. In 1981, he turned lyricist with Yash Chopra's *Silsila*, and is today considered among India's leading and most versatile lyricists, writing songs for films as diverse as *Dil Chahta Hai, Lagaan, Kal Ho Na Ho,* and *Zindagi Na Milegi Dobara.* In 2010, Javed Akhtar was nominated to the Rajya Sabha (Upper House) by the president of India. Through Akhtar's initiative and efforts, the Rajya Sabha passed an amendment to the original Indian Copyright Bill of 1957 that now includes the rights of lyricists, music composers, and singers. He has also served as the vice-president of the International Confederation of Societies of Authors and Composers.

A highly respected social commentator, Javed Akhtar is a leading intellectual, television presenter, and the author of three collections of Urdu poetry, *Tarkash, Lava,* and *In Other Words.*

Born in India, **Nasreen Munni Kabir** is a renowned UK-based
documentary film-maker who has produced and directed over
80 TV programmes on Hindi cinema for Channel 4 TV, UK,
including the series *Movie Mahal*, *In Search of Guru Dutt*, *Lata in
Her Own Voice*, and the two-part documentary *The Inner and Outer
World of Shah Rukh Khan*. She has also directed a profile on Ustad
Bismillah Khan and on the making of *Bombay Dreams*, the musical
produced by Andrew Lloyd Webber for BBC Television, UK.
She continues to curate Channel 4's annual Indian film seasons.

Author of 16 books on Hindi cinema, Nasreen has served on the
board of the British Film Institute for a six-year term. She enjoys
subtitling, and has subtitled over 500 Hindi films. Her last book
was *Conversations with Waheeda Rehman*. She is most remembered
for her Guru Dutt biography, titled *Guru Dutt: A Life in Cinema*
(OUP, 1996). Nasreen continues live in London.